Popular Med

WHEN
CHANGING
A LIGHTBULB
JUST ISN'T ENOUGH

EMILY ANDERSON

Popular Mechanics

WHEN CHANGING A LIGHTBULB JUST ISN'T ENOUGH

EMILY ANDERSON

HEARST BOOKS

A division of Sterling Publishing Co., Inc.

New York / London

www.sterlingpublishing.com

Book Design by Liana Zamora

Library of Congress Cataloging-in-Publication Data available upon request.

10 9 8 7 6 5 4 3 2 1

Published by Hearst Books
A Division of Sterling Publishing Co., Inc.
387 Park Avenue South, New York, NY 10016

Popular Mechanics and Hearst Books are trademarks of Hearst Communications, Inc.

www.popularmechanics.com

For information about custom editions, special sales, premium and corporate purchases,
please contact Sterling Special Sales Department at 800-805-5489 or
specialsales@sterlingpublishing.com.

Distributed in Canada by Sterling Publishing
c/o Canadian Manda Group, 165 Dufferin Street
Toronto, Ontario, Canada M6K 3H6

Distributed in Australia by Capricorn Link (Australia) Pty. Ltd.
P.O. Box 704, Windsor, NSW 2756 Australia

Manufactured in China

Sterling ISBN 978-1-58816-748-4

CONTENTS

FOREWORD

The Editors of Popular Mechanics

It's been more than two decades since the infamous Mobro 4000 garbage barge cruised the East Coast of the United States for six months, searching for a place to unload. In the intervening years, we proved our ability to make great environmental changes.

The first federal standards for water-efficient plumbing fixtures rolled out in 1992, halting the rapid increase in indoor water use. After nearly doubling between 1960 and 1990, today's per capita garbage production holds steady at 4.5 pounds per day. Innovative government-backed programs like Energy Star now help families lower their energy bills by a third by steering them toward energy-efficient appliances.

Small changes can have a big impact. And that's what this book will teach you: the small changes that will not only help you reduce your eco-footprint, but also help lower your cost of living. You don't need to spend a small fortune retrofitting your house to save on your electricity, gas, and water bills.

Big energy leaks often hide in plain sight, and many of them are easy to fix—you may not even need tools. Simply adding attic insulation and weatherstripping slashed bills in one home in Austin, Texas by 60 percent. We'll teach you how to conduct an energy audit to sniff out those trouble spots.

If the price of water was anything like the price of gasoline, nobody would leave the tap running while they brush their teeth. While water-saving efforts may not have the same financial impact that energy conservation has, increasingly more areas of the world—including parts of the U.S.—now suffer from either extreme drought or water-quality issues.

Despite the growth of recycling programs, the U.S. still contributes 133 million tons of garbage to its landfills every year. Scarily, that number includes 25 percent of all food purchased, or 96 billion pounds of leftovers. Yet simply planning your meals more carefully could avoid food waste and feed your family for an entire week each month.

Within these pages, we'll share dozens of small changes that can help pad your wallet while conserving our environment's limited resources. Added together, even small changes can have big results. Turn the page and start trimming your utility bills today.

The Editors
Popular Mechanics

INTRODUCTION

Save Green by Going Green

There are plenty of environmental reasons to go green, from reducing global warming to saving an endangered species. But here's one you may not have considered: green choices mean more money in your wallet. Everything from selecting the fuel that will heat our house to the cars and home appliances we buy impacts the environment, and more often than not, the more eco-friendly the choice, the more you'll save. →

10 EASY STEPS TO A GOOD GREEN START

When it's time to make that improvement on your house—and help the environment and reduce your utility bills at the same time—it can be difficult to figure out just where to begin. Follow these ten easy steps designed to get you off to a great start.

1. Get Organized

Your many house, yard or cleaning projects can make for unnecessary clutter and confusion. Make sure to set aside and group your tools, materials and tasks for each project. Try to keep everything separate from start to cleanup.

2. Buy a Clipboard

Keep all your sketches and shopping lists in one place. You want to be ready to buy everything at once.

3. Don't Leave Organization for Saturday

It's easy and tempting to put off all the work until the weekend, but during the week, check the tools you'll need and their necessary bits, blades and abrasives. You don't want to waste time making extra trips to the hardware store. If you're building, make a neat sketch and figure out your materials beforehand. Plan the project steps and make notes. Make sure to inspect anything you plan to remove or repair. No one wants any last-minute surprises.

4. Start Early

Sleeping in might be one of the joys of the weekend, but when you've got large projects that require daylight, starting early ensures that you get the job done on time.

5. Begin With the Heavy Part

Do the hardest work in the morning, when you're still refreshed and full of energy. By the end of the day, you'll probably be too tired to do any heavy lifting or thinking.

6. Don't Rush

Rushing a job might give you the chance to enjoy more of your weekend. But if you make mistakes, you'll

sink, both supply lines, and the drain.

9. Always Make a Plan B
Because things rarely go as planned, make a Plan B. Start out with a small repair on a toilet and before you know it, you're remodeling your bathroom. If that toilet is the only one in the house, you've got trouble.

10. Cut to the Chase
You have to be ruthless when you do repair and remodeling work. For example, if you were prepared to simply unthread some rusty old plumbing, you might find yourself struggling for an hour just to get the stuff apart. In that case, you would be better off just slicing the parts off with a reciprocating saw and starting from scratch. Wrestling with old components that have outlived their service life is a waste of time. We hope the projects and ideas in this book will help you spring into action, because your small changes can make a big difference.

spend more time fixing them later.

7. Remember That You Don't Do This Stuff Every Day
Unless you're a home improvement contractor, you have to expect that a job will take a lot longer than you thought it would. Don't get too frustrated and give yourself more than enough time to finish your projects.

8. Expect the Worst
When you're dealing with old plumbing and electrical, problems typically run a lot deeper than anticipated. Expect the worst and be prepared to do more work than required. You won't be disappointed. Example: Recently, I went to change a washer in an old faucet. Before the day was done, I had replaced the faucet, the

→ It's difficult to comprehend that your choice of a car can make a change on a global level, but it does—and approaching the process with small steps means everyone can pitch in. No one can deny that we are using up natural resources at an alarming rate. From forests to water to fish and wildlife, our choices are causing some big problems. What we do today will most certainly impact us tomorrow. With fuel prices eating into our budgets, water shortages leaving our lawns brown, and overtaxed power grids causing rolling blackouts, every environmental challenge has a direct economic corollary.

The cornerstone of good eco-policy is recycling and reusing, which applies to what we consume, what we throw away, and how we spend our money. In this book are dozens of small changes you can make that in turn will make a huge difference—in essence, saving the world and your pocketbook at the same time.

3 EASY GREEN WAYS TO SAVE MONEY

1 DRIVE LESS

Driving your car less isn't just good for the environment. With gas costing more and more, it's not unreasonable to expect to spend hundreds of dollars a month just driving around town. Carpooling, telecommuting, and combining trips to the store are just three ways to drive less and keep your cash where it belongs—in the bank.

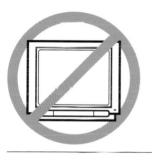

2 TURN OFF YOUR TV

Television uses almost 300 watts of energy every hour it's on, and the average household watches four hours each day. Cut back on the boob tube and toss around a pigskin with the family instead—your utility bill won't be the only thing that improves.

3 GO TO A SWAP MEET

Before you toss something in the trash, think about how it might be useful to you reused in another way. If you can't think of anything, find a local swap meet and trade your item for something else, or barter it away online. (freecycle.com)

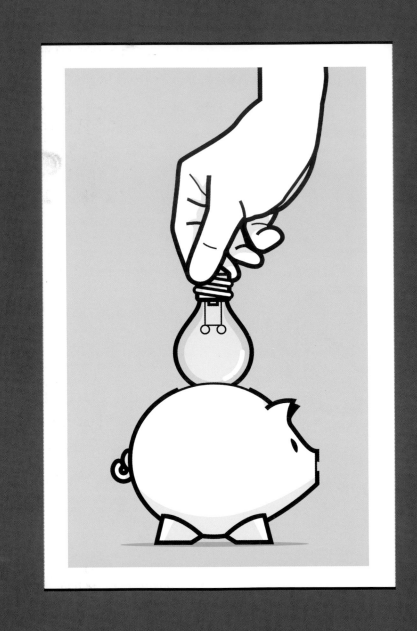

SAVE RESOURCES, SAVE MONEY

→ There are many ways to reduce your home's energy footprint, and the savings can be substantial, both in cash and in emissions of greenhouse gases. A typical home emits almost 9,000 pounds of carbon dioxide per person per year—altogether, residences make up about 17 percent of America's CO_2 emissions.

↓ WHERE DOES IT ALL GO?
HERE'S A BREAKDOWN OF YOUR HOUSEHOLD ENERGY USE BASED ON DATA* FROM THE DEPARTMENT OF ENERGY:

IF YOU HAVE:	EACH YEAR YOU USE:		IF YOU HAVE:	EACH YEAR YOU USE:	
HEATING		46.9%	**HEATING WATER**		17%
ELECTRIC	3,517 KWH		ELECTRICITY	2,550 KWH	
NATURAL GAS	16,237 KWH		NATURAL GAS	5,774 KWH	
	(55.4 MILLION BTU)			(19.7 MILLION BTU)	
FUEL OIL	20,574 KWH		FUEL OIL	8,236 KWH	
	(70.2 MILLION BTU)			(28.1 MILLION BTU)	
AIR CONDITIONING		6.3%	**APPLIANCES**		29.8%
CENTRAL AIR CONDITIONING	2,796 KWH		REFRIGERATOR	1,462 KWH	
2 ROOM AIR CONDITIONING	1,160 KWH		LIGHTING	940 KWH	
			MICROWAVE OVEN	209 KWH	
			WASHER AND DRYER	1,199 KWH	
			PLASMA TELEVISION	166 KWH	
			DESKTOP COMPUTER	318 KWH	

* Note: A fuel's energy content typically is shown in British thermal units (BTUs). To make comparisons among appliances easier, we list kilowatt-hour equivalents. 1 kwh = 3413 BTU.

Heating and Cooling

Heating consumes more energy than anything else in the home, accounting for almost 47 percent of the nation's residential energy use. But not so long ago, America's home energy picture was enviable. In the late 1970s and early 1980s, consumption plummeted as homeowners took steps such as adding insulation and caulking around windows. But all that changed in the years following the early 1990s, when the average size of a new house increased from 1,500 sq. ft. to nearly 2,500 sq. ft. Knowing where you waste energy will help you take the steps necessary to trim your energy bills.

► WEEKEND PROJECT

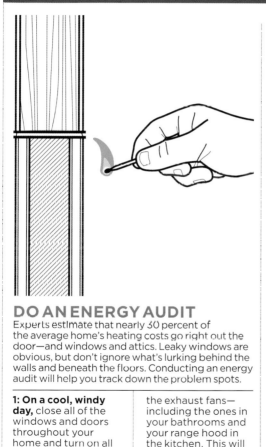

slightly depressurize your house and increase airflow between the inside and outside.

2: Light a match and blow it out. (You can also do this with a lit stick of incense). Walk through each room, moving the incense anywhere you feel there might be a problem: along the window and door frames, baseboards, switch plates, and along the sill plate in the basement.

3: Watch the smoke. If it's dragged toward the outside or blown back into the room, you have found a leak. Use painter's tape to mark the area(s) so you can go back to fix them.

DO AN ENERGY AUDIT

Experts estimate that nearly 30 percent of the average home's heating costs go right out the door—and windows and attics. Leaky windows are obvious, but don't ignore what's lurking behind the walls and beneath the floors. Conducting an energy audit will help you track down the problem spots.

1: On a cool, windy day, close all of the windows and doors throughout your home and turn on all the exhaust fans—including the ones in your bathrooms and your range hood in the kitchen. This will

Cost: None
Monthly Savings: $15
Payback: Immediate

PROGRAM YOUR THERMOSTAT

A good programmable thermostat for your heating and cooling system will cost between $50 and $150, depending on the features you want. Look for a thermostat with a backup battery in case of a power outage, and the abilities to store multiple settings and manually change the temperature without affecting the preprogrammed data. Keep in mind that you'll need to reduce the temperature for at least eight hours (either at night or while you're at work) to see a noticeable energy savings.

TOOLS AND MATERIALS

- Screwdriver
- Wire cutters/strippers
- Pencil
- Masking tape
- Level
- Drill
- $^3/_{16}$-in. drill bit

Cost: $42
Monthly Savings: $15
Payback: 3 months

1: Turn off the power to the surrounding circuit and the circuit for the furnace and air conditioner. Install the batteries in the new thermostat.

2: Unscrew and remove the old thermostat's mounting plate from the wall. The old thermostat should have a letter identifying each wire. Attach the labels included with your new thermostat to each wire, corresponding to the letters on the old thermostat.

3: Once the wires are marked, disconnect the old thermostat, making sure the wires don't fall back into the wall. Wrap the wires around your pencil to keep them in place.

QUICK
FIX

4: Position the new
thermostat base
against the wall to make
sure it sits flush and
none of the wires are
trapped behind it. Level
the base, then mark the
center of the mounting
plate's screw holes.

5: Remove the base
and drill a $3/16$-in.-
diameter hole at each
screw location. Use a
hammer to gently tap
plastic anchors into the
holes; reposition the
thermostat over the
anchors.

6: Thread the wires
from the wall through
the base of the new
thermostat, then insert
and tighten the mounting
screws. Connect the
wires to the screw
terminals according
to the manufacturer's
instructions, matching
the labels to the letters
on the terminals. (You
may need to strip the
wires first.)

7: Turn the electricity
back on at the service
panel, and test the
thermostat—in both
the auto and manual
modes—to confirm
that the furnace and
air conditioner cycle
on and off at the
appropriate settings.

CHANGE YOUR PLAN
Improve efficiency
by changing the
times you use
electricity. New
rules require utilities
to offer optional
"time-of-use" rate
plans, in which the
price of electricity
varies with the time
of day. Because
power costs as little
as one-third as much
at night, there's
a real advantage
to running large
appliances, such
as dishwashers and
washing machines,
after dark.

BE AN ENERGY STAR

The Energy Star program, sponsored by the Environmental Protection Agency (EPA) and the Department of Energy (DOA), helps to reduce greenhouse gas emissions through energy-efficient products and practices. Appliances carrying the Energy Star rating are typically 20 to 30 percent more energy efficient than nonrated models, although specifications will differ from item to item. As you upgrade or replace appliances, check for the Energy Star label to see instant savings on your energy costs—and add value to your home. Many home buyers now request that Energy Star appliances be included in their purchasing contract.

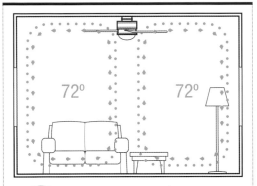

QUICK FIX

USE FANS

Window, ceiling, and floor fans can keep you cool enough for comfort, especially during the nighttime hours. Window and ceiling fans require just 10 percent of the energy used by air conditioners. Keep the fan blades clean of dust to maximize their effectiveness.

> **WEEKEND PROJECT**

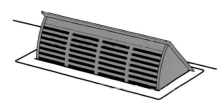

REGISTER BASICS

Registers can be a helpful tool in optimizing your heating and cooling system. Check around your house and make some adjustments.

1: Guest rooms, bathrooms, and any other rooms that are seldom used should be "closed off" for the winter or summer. This also includes under-insulated rooms, such as an enclosed porch. Make sure the registers in these parts of the house are closed tight.

2: Arrange furnishings so they don't cover heating and cooling registers. Check to see if anything is obstructing the natural flow of the warm or cool air, such as a sofa or drapes.

3: Add pop-up heat deflectors to direct air; this is especially helpful if you have long drapes that sit on top of your register vent. You can pop up the deflectors, which cost less than $10, as needed. For a more permanent solution, add scoop-shaped deflectors for less than $2 each.

Cost: $50 for 10 pop-up deflectors
Monthly Savings: $4
Payback: 12.5 months

> **QUICK FIX**

CLOSE THE FIREPLACE FLUE

On average, 14 percent of the air leaking in and out of a house flows through the chimney. Make it a habit to close the fireplace damper whenever it is not being used. Be sure to open the flue before lighting a fire in the fireplace. If you use your fireplace infrequently, seal it with an inflatable draft stopper or make your own with a garbage bag stuffed with fiberglass insulation.

QUICK FIX

CHANGE THE TEMPERATURE

In the winter, dropping the indoor temperature 1 degree at night and during work hours can cut heating costs up to 3 percent, according to the American Institute of Architects (AIA). Doing the reverse with the air conditioning in the summer will save up to 6 percent. The most efficient temperature during the winter is between 68 and 70°F. In the summer months, keep the air conditioner thermostat between 76 and 78°F.

QUICK FIX

PULL THE SHADES

During the summer, open windows wide during the cooler evening hours, but keep the shades down during the sunniest part of the day to block heat-causing rays and retain air conditioning. During the winter, use drapes to help keep out the drafts.

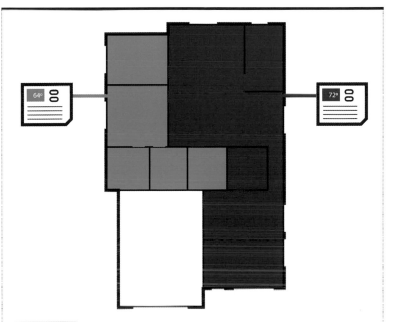

USE ZONE HEATING AND COOLING

FUTURE INVESTMENT

Only some rooms are in use at any given time: the living room, study, and kitchen during the day; the bedroom at night. Zone heating and cooling contains the hot or cool air only in the sections you are using. While the cost of a zone heating and cooling system can be expensive, a properly zoned heating and cooling system is controlled by multiple thermostats located in various parts of your home, and can be up to 30 percent more efficient than a nonzoned system. One such system was developed by EnerZone Systems, funded by the U.S. Department of Energy's Inventions and Innovation Program, which developed a method for selectively controlling airflow to rooms in the home from a central HVAC system. (retrozone.com)

INSTALL AN ATTIC FAN

During the summer, the temperature in an attic can reach 150°F, which accounts for 20 percent of the average home's cooling bill. Available with humidistats as well as thermostats, an attic fan can control excess attic humidity during the colder months. This project is for the installation of a gable-wall fan. If your attic is excessively hot, you will benefit from a roof fan and should consult a licensed contractor, as it will require structural changes to your roof.

TOOLS AND MATERIALS

- A gable-vent fan
- Screwdriver
- Hammer
- Plywood (cut to fit the size of your fan)
- Caulk
- Sabre saw

1. Remove the old gable vent by loosening the screws or removing the nails with a hammer.

2. Hold the shutter face against the siding, and trace around it. Measure in $5/8$ in. to establish the new opening.

3. If any nonstructural blocking obstructs the opening, cut through the nails with a reciprocating saw and remove. Use a sabre saw to enlarge the opening to its new size.

4. Screw the automatic shutter over the opening and seal the perimeter with an acrylic caulk. Lift the new shutter into the opening, double-check that it's level, and fasten it in place with 1-in. woodscrews.

5. Nail the old blocking in place just below the bottom of the shutter. Replace any blocking you cut out when enlarging the opening.

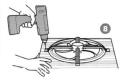

8. Place the fan mounting bracket on the plywood, center the fan over the opening and screw the bracket to the

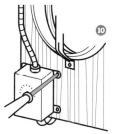

6. Cut a piece of plywood on which to mount the fan. Next, cut a cardboard circle template from the fan carton and use it to mark the airway hole on the plywood mounting panel.

7. Use a sabre saw to cut the airway in the mounting panel. Bore a hole in the waste area to start the cut.

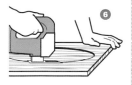

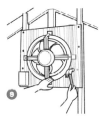

plywood. Back them with washers to keep them from pulling through.

9. The fan assembly needs to be oriented vertically, so look for the Up/Down markings on one set of supports and mark the top of the plywood mounting panel accordingly. Carry

the fan and panel assembly into the attic, position it behind the shutter, and nail it to the gable framing.

10. How you wire your attic fan will depend on local codes and whether you can find an attic circuit with enough reserve capacity to handle the 3.2-amp fan motor. Unless you are experienced with electrical work, hire an electrician to ensure everything is done safely.

Cost: $150

Monthly Savings: $15 during the summer

Payback: 10 months

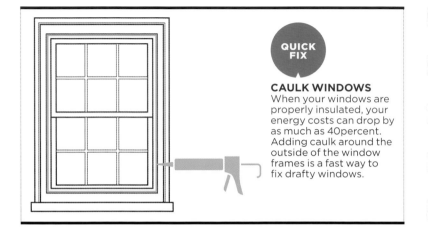

QUICK FIX

CAULK WINDOWS

When your windows are properly insulated, your energy costs can drop by as much as 40percent. Adding caulk around the outside of the window frames is a fast way to fix drafty windows.

QUICK FIX

DON'T BE UNDER-INSULATED

Attics are huge energy drains. Use loose-fill cellulose insulation to quickly reduce heat loss in under-insulated and old attics. It is blown under the flooring and between the floor joists. If you plan to turn the attic into living space, install fiberglass insulation between the rafters while leaving an air space between it and the roof deck.

► **WEEKEND PROJECT**

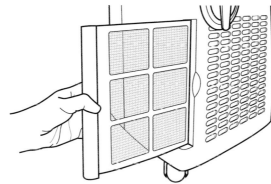

BE COOL

Central air conditioning is far more efficient than window air conditioners, but expensive ($6,000 to over $15,000, depending on its seasonal energy efficiency rating and the size of your home). If you have window units, here are a few ways to optimize performance and lower energy costs.

1: Use the recirculate option on window air conditioners. It takes much less energy to cool air that is already relatively cool than to cool hot exterior air.

2: Clean the filters regularly. When in use, air conditioner filters need to be cleaned at least every two weeks. Just vacuum out the filter and reinstall. Your air will be cleaner and your air conditioner won't have to work as hard.

3: A new energy-efficient air conditioner should have an energy efficiency rating of at least 10. By swapping an older room unit you can cut costs by 20 percent.

4: Use a timer to control when the air is on. If you don't have a timer built into your unit, use a programmable wall outlet timer.

5: Lower the fan setting. The unit will remove more humidity, boosting comfort while saving energy.

Cost: From $0 to $600 (for a new air conditioner)
Monthly Savings: $8 to $30
Payback: Variable

PROBE UTILITY BILLS

Pay careful attention to the pattern of your bills. Keep track of weather on a calendar, making note of changes between weekends and weekdays. Your utility bills can reveal patterns of energy usage—and help you track the savings from upgrades.

TIPS OF THE TRADE:
DRAFTY ATTIC STAIRWAYS

The attic might be sealed tight and insulated to R-39, but you've overlooked a gaping, 21-sq ft. hole that's hemorrhaging money: the pull-down stairs. An easy and effective solution is to construct a rigid insulation cover for the stairway. In addition to reducing drafts, the cover will reduce heat loss through that area.

Pre-made covers exist, or you can build your own from rigid polystyrene insulation. The top of the cover should be large enough to overlap the perimeter of the stairway opening by a couple of inches. The sides must be deep enough to accommodate the folding stairway in its closed position. Once the top and four sides are cut to size, they can be attached to one another with a multipurpose construction adhesive. Use duct tape to apply clamping force.

Be careful: the solvent in some adhesives will react with Styrofoam. Be sure the product you buy is compatible with the material you're gluing. While you're waiting for your new cover to dry, weatherstrip the hatch.

A 1-in.-thick Styrofoam board has a thermal resistance (R-factor) of about 5. If you'd like greater thermal resistance, then either double up on the Styrofoam or insulate the cover with Fiberglas batts. Since the cover will weigh only a few pounds, it can easily be moved around when you use the stairway.

WEEKEND PROJECT

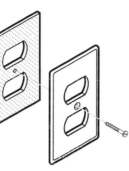

INSULATE SWITCH PLATES AND ELECTRICAL OUTLETS

Insulating your outlets takes little time and next to no money. Simply install inexpensive foam gaskets (available at hardware stores) behind drafty switch plates and electrical outlets on exterior walls.

1: Remove the outlet or switch plate cover using the screwdriver.

2: Slip the foam piece over the outlet and replace the outlet cover.

TOOLS AND MATERIALS

Cost: $10 for 10 gaskets
Monthly Savings: $1 to $4
Payback: 3 to 6 months

- Screwdriver
- Several foam gasket/covers (shaped like outlet covers)

QUICK FIX

PLUG BIG GAPS

Practice triage by stopping the big energy bleeders—large, obvious breaches in the basement and attic—before caulking cracks or insulating. Prime offenders are gaps at plumbing stacks, furnace flues, and stud cavities inside soffits. Plug holes with expanding foam, foil-backed foam board, or fiberglass insulation scraps stuffed in a plastic garbage bag to stop air movement. Use heat-resistant caulk and sheet-metal around chimney flues and combustion vents.

GREEN MORTGAGE

If you're looking to buy a home or refinance your current one, consider an energy-efficient mortgage (EEM). Originally created in 1979, these mortgages allow you to use your commitment to the environment to leverage a bigger loan by folding the costs of energy improvements into the borrowed amount. Up to 15percent of the home's future appraised value is held in escrow to cover the cost of energy upgrades. If you are purchasing a new home, ask your builder to provide a Home Energy Rating System (HERS) report that states the house meets energy-efficiency guidelines. A rating is required to apply for both new mortgages and a refinancing, and usually costs less than $500.

COVER AIR DUCT JOINTS

Open joints and inadequate insulation in ducts are major sources of wasted energy, especially when the metal ducts are in a crawlspace. Duct insulation is usually marginal and additional insulation is typically needed. Call a professional if you notice any red flags—such as damaged or dislodged ducts or duct tape used as a structural joint fastener—which can melt from attic and crawlspace heat and release.

1: Use your flashlight to identify air duct joints in your crawlspace. Check for non obvious leakage by wetting the palm of your hand and holding it over the suspected area. If there is a leak, you will feel a cool sensation on your palm.

2: Following the directions given by the duct mastic's manufacturer, brush or smear the mastic on the duct joints, using the mesh tape as its base. It should dry in minutes.

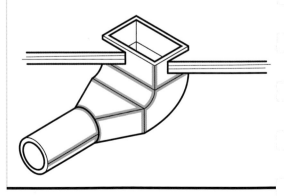

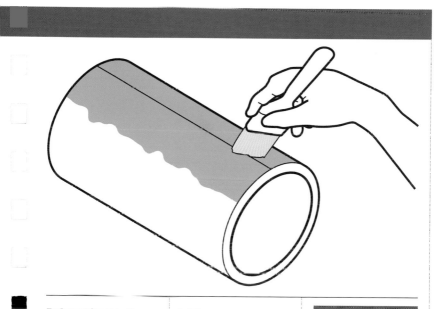

3: Once the mastic has dried into a hard, permanent seal, wrap insulation around the ducts securely. Log onto the U.S. Department of Energy's Zip-Code Insulation Program for assistance in the selection of the proper insulation. (ornl.gov/~roofs/Zip/ZipHome.html)

4: Wrap a vapor barrier, such as polyethylene sheets with edges overlapped and taped together with heavy-duty plastic tape, around the insulation to prevent condensation from forming when the air conditioning is running.

Cost: $40

Monthly Savings: $9.33

Payback: 4 months

TOOLS AND MATERIALS

- Duct mastic, available as a liquid or paste
- Mesh tape
- Flashlight
- Medium paintbrush
- Formaldehyde-free insulation
- 4- or 6-mil polyethylene sheets
- Heavy-duty plastic tape

WEATHERSTRIPPING

Adding weather stripping to your windows is one of the easiest and least expensive ways to stop air infiltration. While many newer windows include factory-installed weather stripping, it may not be of the best quality. Bear in mind that with older, single-glazed (single-pane) windows, you could lose up to twice as much heat as you would with double-glazed windows. The difference is even more striking with triple glazing, which is about five times as efficient as single glazing.

Cost: $10 per window
Monthly Savings: $2.15 per window
Payback: 5 months

1: Spring-type, tension, or folded weather strips are commonly made from bronze, aluminum, stainless steel, or vinyl. Best for use on double-hung windows and doors, these angled or V-shaped strips seal well and cannot be seen when the window or door is closed. When installing, nail directly to the window frame except at the bottom, where you will nail to the sash.

2: Pliable-gasket weather strips made from vinyl, felt, or foam attached to wood or metal strips. Effective for use with wood casement, hinged, and sliding windows, they are attached at the bottom or top of the window sash and may be painted after installation to reduce visibility. While durability varies, it is generally low, and the self-adhesive strips may not work effectively on metal.

3: The least durable option are compressible felt strips. Use only with warped windows that won't accept more rigid stripping or are seldom opened.

TOOLS AND MATERIALS

- Utility knife
- Tape measure
- Hammer
- Weather stripping

KNOW YOUR STUFF:
FAULTY DOUBLE-PANED
GLASS WINDOWS

If your double-pane glass windows or sliding doors have clouded up, it's because of a faulty seal between the two panes of glass. Unfortunately, it's not a do-it-yourself project.

Double- and triple-glazed windows have an airtight seal between the panes. This is achieved under carefully controlled conditions at a factory, and it's unlikely the steps can be replicated at home. To repair a faulty window you have to remove the existing seal, clean out the edge joints so that a new seal can be applied, replace the dessicant in the spacer, clean the panes, and reassemble the window unit. The airspace between the panes is filled with argon or air at atmospheric pressure—it is not under a vacuum. Argon, which is inert and chemically inactive, is used more often than air because it has a lower thermal conductivity. This means it has a greater resistance to heat flow.

Don't worry, however. Even though the seal has failed, the window will still serve an energy-saving function. It is still more effective than a single-glazed window and is probably comparable to a storm window. And there's even better news: depending on how old your window is, you may be able to get a replacement from the manufacturer. Most manufacturers guarantee their products for five to ten years against failure caused by a faulty seal. They will replace a pane at no cost within the warranty's time limit. Some manufacturers have longer warranties.

When properly made, insulated glass windows will last many years. Because windows are an important part of your home, they should never be purchased strictly on price. It's better to buy windows that are made by a manufacturer that has been in business long enough to justify confidence in its product and that backs its product with a substantial warranty.

LOOK UP

If you have ventilation problems, your roof will let you know. Common signs of an overly hot attic are asphalt shingles with their corners curled up, or bulges in the felt and shingles directly over the seams in the sheathing. Inadequate venting leads to high attic temperatures that can reduce comfort, raise utility bills, and shorten the useful life of roofing materials. On cold winter days, look for frost inside the attic. This frost is trapped moisture that can rot the entire roof if it is not allowed to escape.

SAFE AND SOUND:
OIL HEATING TANKS

If you keep your house heated via a buried oil heating tank (such as a 550-gal. tank), be aware that a leaking tank should be a major concern. The cost for excavation, carting, and dumping contaminated soil in an EPA-approved site can cost thousands or even tens of thousands of dollars, and can exceed $100,000 depending on how much soil is contaminated.

Keep a close eye on your oil-consumption records, but be aware that small leaks (such as a gallon a year) can easily be overlooked. Some tanks have been known to leak after only five years. Steel tanks usually last 15 to 20 years, although many tanks last longer. It's advisable to get older tanks tested for leakage. You might have to make several phone calls to get information on buried oil tanks. Start with your state's environmental agency.

WEEKEND PROJECT

INSTALL A RUBBER DOOR SWEEP

Cost: $10 per door
Monthly Savings: $2.15 per door
Payback: 5 months

An airtight seal installed on the bottom of any door that leads outside—or to areas that aren't temperature controlled, such as the garage—will reduce drafts and improve your home's heat retention. A wide variety of sweeps are available for every kind of door, including storm doors and roll-up garage doors. If the threshold is above the level of the floor or carpeting, the simplest solution is a rubber door sweep. In order to completely weatherproof a door, weather stripping should be installed on the sides and top of the doorframe.

TOOLS AND MATERIALS

- Rubber door sweep
- Adhesive-backed weather stripping
- Power drill
- Screwdriver
- Utility knife

1: Thoroughly clean the door frame and tighten all hinge screws. Measure the door frame and cut strips slightly larger than size.

2: Slowly peel off the adhesive backing and press strip into place in sections. Trim to size where necessary, and pay close attention to where the weather stripping on the side abuts the top strip.

3: With the door closed, screw the sweep to the bottom of the door. Placement is crucial; the sweep should seal the threshold but still allow the door to easily open and close.

Hot Water

About 58 million homes heat their water with gas, while 42 million use electricity. But electric systems account for about 50 percent more carbon emissions, because so much power is lost in generation and transmission. The U.S. Environmental Protection Agency reports that the typical American uses 100 gallons of water each day. Trimming usage should be your top priority, but you can also install solar hot-water heaters or "on-demand" heaters, which have no storage tank and are 30 percent more efficient.

SAVE RESOURCES, SAVE MONEY

TAKE SHOWERS, NOT BATHS

A five-minute shower uses 10 gal. of hot water, half as much as a bath if you have a low-flow showerhead. Set an egg timer to remind you when it's time to get out.

NIGHT WISE

Put a timer on your electric water heater that turns it off while you're asleep or keeps it off during peak hours—especially if you sign up for time-of-use pricing.

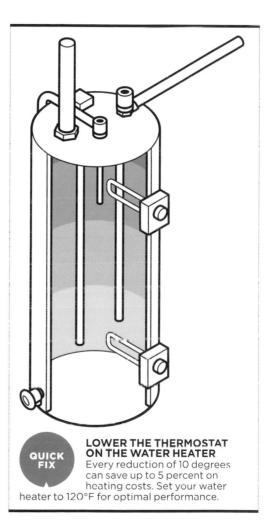

LOWER THE THERMOSTAT ON THE WATER HEATER

Every reduction of 10 degrees can save up to 5 percent on heating costs. Set your water heater to 120°F for optimal performance.

TIPS OF THE TRADE:
INSTALL A WATER SOFTENER

If your dishes have water spots and your faucets, fixtures, and showerheads accumulate scale, you need to install a water softener. When minerals precipitate on external surfaces, they're doing the same inside your pipes. Scale accumulations in pipes eventually restrict flow. In water heaters, scaly sediment increases energy consumption and shortens tank life. Hard water also has trouble dissolving soaps—enough that a softener can cut your detergent use in half.

Hard water contains too much calcium and magnesium, which is absorbed as it percolates through rock and gravel aquifers. Hardness is measured in grains per gallon (GPG). Rainwater has no hardness, or zero grains, but most of us can live with 1 to 10 GPG. If you're a diligent housekeeper, even 11 to 18 GPG may be manageable. In this range, the effects can be aggravating but it would take a lifetime for the mineral buildup to close pipes.

Anything above about 18 grains is a real problem, however, in terms of both plumbing damage and soap use. To determine your water's hardness, collect a few ounces in a clean container and take it to your local water-equipment company. Testing is usually free.

In a water softener, the water passes through a tank that's filled with porous plastic beads of polyester resin called zeolite. When treated with a salt solution, usually sodium chloride, the beads attract sodium ions from the salt. When hard water is sent through the bead-filled tank, magnesium and calcium ions trade places with the sodium. Eventually, in a few days or a week, the resin loads up with minerals and is flushed with fresh salt water. Most communities allow brine purges into public sewers, but if yours doesn't, you'll need a removal service. Well-designed septic systems are not harmed by brine purges.

The primary difference between water softener models is in the way they schedule the purging cycles. This is important because recharging the beads with salt too early wastes salt and water. Recharging too late causes performance to fall off.

The most affordable softeners use timers to estimate the point of saturation. The problem is, actual water use varies from week to week. Midprice softeners go one better by including flow meters. These are programmed to recharge and purge when a given volume of water passes through the system. They come close to being exact, especially when paired with microprocessors that factor in ongoing user habits. The best softeners use probes in the resin tank to detect the exact point of saturation.

Water softeners are installed in the main water trunk line, before any branch lines, to treat the entire indoor supply system. For economy reasons, outdoor faucets are repiped to the main line before the water softener, so they'll continue to deliver untreated water. A bypass valve, required by code, allows you to skip the water softener if it's ever necessary to do so. If you or one of your household is on a low-sodium diet, consider installing a dedicated drinking-water tap to supply untreated, sodium-free water to the kitchen, and connect your refrigerator's icemaker to that line. As an alternative, potassium chloride may be suitable for your situation.

REPLACE YOUR DISHWASHER

When it's time to upgrade your dishwasher, buy one with a built-in booster heater so you can lower the thermostat on your main water heater and still get good results. Be prepared to purchase one with a higher price tag; the long-term savings will be worth it.

QUICK FIX

WASH WITH THE COLD CYCLE

Launder only full loads. Up to 85 percent of the energy consumed when washing clothes is used to heat the water. The difference in cost between the Cold/Cold and Hot/Hot cycles can be as much as 60 cents per load and cold water works just as well, especially with cold-water detergents. Only use warm water when it's absolutely necessary.

QUICK FIX

FILL YOUR DISHWASHER

Only run your dishwasher when it is totally full, and don't pre-rinse if you have a newer machine. Run on Normal rather than Pots and Pans, and let your dishes air dry.

► **WEEKEND
PROJECT**

FINDING BLANKET SOLUTIONS

If a water heater is warm to the touch, it is wasting power. A homeowner's simplest solution is to add a fiberglass insulation blanket. Many companies now use eco-friendly recycled glass in their fiberglass insulation products.

1: For an electric heater, just cut holes in the fiberglass blanket for the heating element covers. With gas heaters, be careful not to block airflow to the burner. Use tape to secure it on the sides and top.

2: Insulate the pipes with sleeves, particularly within 3 ft. of the storage tank

3: Heat loss also occurs through the convective flow of hot water into the pipes. Install the heat trap of your choice to stop the flow.

TOOLS AND MATERIALS

- Thermal fiberglass insulation blanket
- Preformed insulation tubes
- Heat traps (one-way valves or loops of flexible pipe)
- Utility knife
- Tape

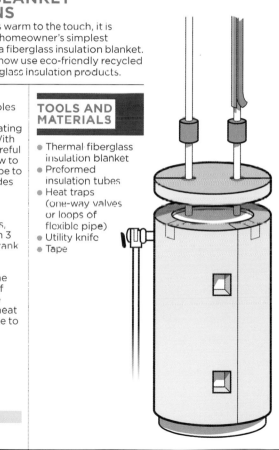

Cost: $30
Monthly Savings: $1.20
Payback: 25 months

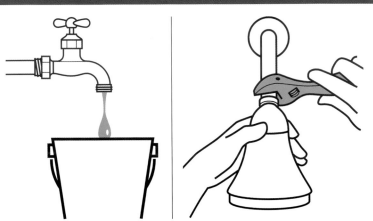

USE LOW-FLOW SHOWERHEADS AND FAUCET AERATORS

Fill a bucket in your shower. If it takes less than 20 seconds to reach 1 gal., install a low-flow showerhead. There are two basic kinds available. An aerating showerhead mixes water into the water stream, maintaining steady pressure and an even spray. Non aerating showerheads use a pulsating system to reduce water flow, which feels like a massaging showerhead.

The same concept applies to faucets elsewhere in your home. A faucet aerator can save 400 gal. of hot water per year. Translation: less work for the water heater. If the rated flow on your current aerator is visible, and if it's above 2.75 gal./minute, then replace it with a more efficient model that emits 1.5 gal./minute or less. If the aerator's flow rate has been scuffed off or it's too hard to read, just replace it. The new aerator will likely have lower flow.

Cost: $4.80 for three aerators
Monthly Savings: $0.93
Payback: 5 months

KNOW YOUR STUFF:
A CRASH COURSE ON
WATER HEATERS

If the time has come for you to replace your water heater, consider finding
a water heating system that will not only provide enough hot water but
also that will do so efficiently—saving you money. Check out these handy
tips provided by the U.S. Department of Energy's Energy Efficiency and
Renewable Energy department (EERE).

TYPES OF WATER HEATERS

- **Conventional storage water heaters.** Offers a ready reservoir (storage
tank) of hot water.

- **On demand (tankless or instantaneous) water heaters.** Heats water
directly without the use of a storage tank.

- **Heat pump water heaters.** Moves heat from one place to another
instead of generating heat directly for providing hot water.

- **Solar water heaters.** Uses the sun's heat to provide hot water.

Tankless coil and indirect water heaters. Uses a home's space heating
system to heat water.

SELECTION CRITERIA

- **Fuel type, availability and cost.** The fuel type or energy source you use
for water heating will not only affect the water heater's annual operation
costs but also its size and energy efficiency.

- **Size.** To provide your household with enough hot water and to maximize
efficiency, you need a properly sized water heater.

- **Energy efficiency.** To maximize your energy and cost savings, you want
to know how energy efficient a water heater is before you purchase it.

- **Costs.** Estimate the annual operating costs and compare those costs
with other less or more energy-efficient models.

Standby Power

Unlike water or space heating, a home's total electrical usage is the sum of many footprints, from small to large. You have the TV and computer here, hair dryer and microwave there. On average, idle machines use 11 percent of a home's electricity, drawing energy from the power source even when they are turned off. Want to reduce your electricity bill? Get unplugged.

FUTURE INVESTMENT

ENERGY EFFICIENCY INCENTIVES

Reducing the amount of electricity you use won't just help you save on your monthly bill: it can also pad your wallet with rebates, tax credits, and loans. Here are a few ways to find out whether you are eligible.

● In 2008, Congress passed the Emergency Economic Stabilization Act, which included an extension of the residential tax credits for energy-efficient improvements. Improvements made in the calendar year of 2009 are eligible for a $500 tax credit. (energystar.gov/index.cfm?c=products. pr_tax_credits)

● Search through hundreds of utility and rebate loan programs on the online Database of State Incentives for Renewables & Efficiency. (dsireusa.org)

● Use the Environmental Protection Agency's Partner Information database to search for rebate and tax-credit programs. (energystar.gov/index. cfm?fuseaction=activity_search.opie_search_partner)

● Contact your utility company directly and ask for the efficiency program. It may offer rebates on appliance purchases that meet EnergyStar or Consortium for Energy Efficiency (CEE) standards. (cee1.org)

MEASURE YOUR ELECTRICITY USAGE

Quickly discover how efficient your electronic appliances are with these handy—and inexpensive—tools.

- **Kill-A-Watt from Smarthome,** plugged between an appliance and its outlet, will track the electricity used.
- **The PowerCost Monitor** connects to an electrical meter and displays total household usage (and its cost).
- **The Energy Detective** measures the amount of electricity coming into your home by connecting directly to your circuit breaker panel and transmits that data over to a display unit. It can also track specific circuits.
- **Online savings calculators** (such as those located at energystar.gov) can help homeowners forecast savings by showing what would happen if you upgraded old dishwashers, freezers, and other appliances.

SEALED TIGHT

The seal of your refrigerator door may wear out before it's time to replace the whole thing. If you can close the door on a dollar bill and pull the bill out without resistance, then the door seal is worn and should be replaced.

SAFE AND SOUND:
CHECK YOUR GFCI OUTLET RECEPTACLES

Checking a GFCI outlet receptacle is a simple electrical safety check that might you're your life. It's as easy as pressing its Test button, and that should cut the power to any device that is plugged into the outlet receptacle as well as any additional outlet receptacles that are wired downstream on the same circuit. When you press the Reset button the power should be restored.

However, faulty GFCI receptacles can give a homeowner a false sense of security. Older GFCI may have been damaged from a high-voltage power surge or corrosion and lost its ground-fault protection, yet it will appear to be operating correctly. Electrical equipment company Leviton has introduced a GFCI outlet receptacle that it calls SmartLock (about $10 at hardware stores and home centers). Damaged devices won't reset once tripped, either by a ground fault or a manual check. The device complies with, and even exceeds, new Underwriters Laboratories (UL) requirements specifying that GFCI outlet receptacles be more durable while also being more resistant to nondangerous nuisance tripping.

GFCI OUTLETS: A PRIMER
Some background on GF CI outlet receptacles may be useful. First, you have to know that any outlet is a connector that links the home's electrical system with an electrical device. Electrons move from the house's wiring to the outlet, through the outlet, through the electrical device, then back through the outlet, back through the house's wiring and return to the electrical grid outside the home.

A GFCI outlet receptacle monitors the electrons coming and going through it. They should be equal. If it senses that more electrons are entering than leaving, it means some electrons are leaking out somewhere. This electrical leak is known as a ground fault (hence GFCI: ground fault circuit interrupter)—electrons are flowing into the ground through a fault of some kind. The GFCI senses this fault and cuts off power in a fraction of a second.

The Electrical Safety Foundation promotes the need to not only test GFCI outlets on a regular basis, but also to replace them when they are found to be malfunctioning. For more information, visit the group's Web site at www.electrical-safety.org.

CHECK YOUR REFRIGERATOR TEMPERATURE

Use an outdoor thermometer to make sure your fridge is working properly. According to the Food and Drug Administration, for optimal food storage and to inhibit the growth of bacteria, the refrigerator box should be kept at or slightly below 40°F. Keep the freezer compartment at 0°F to 5°F. If your fridge does not adjust to a new setting within 24 hours, defrost it and scrub it out.

UNPLUGGED

Your countertop microwave is always on standby—and it uses 98 percent of its operating energy while idle. Keep it unplugged and find a different clock for the kitchen.

INSTALL SMART LIGHTS

For safety or convenience, most homeowners leave at least one light on all the time, whether it's the light over the garage door, the front porch, or the bathroom. With a small investment in timers or motion sensors, you can save energy and keep the lights on.

1: Lights on Timers. Just set the schedule and plug your light into the timer. These will give a realistic impression that someone is in the house.

2: Motion Detector Lights. For overhead and floodlights, invest in motion detectors. This is a great solution for driveway and walkway lights—just make sure they are off during the day.

Cost: $20-$50

Monthly Savings: Variable

Payback: Variable

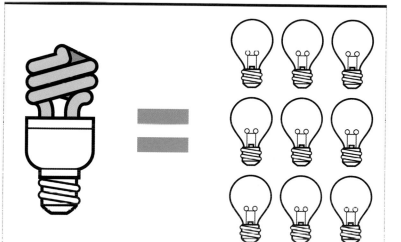

CHANGE A LIGHT BULB

QUICK FIX Compact fluorescent lamps last up to ten times longer than incandescents, generate 90 percent less heat, and require just one quarter of the energy. But before you install, read the fine print. Some bulbs are meant to be used only in downward-facing fixtures, others in enclosed and recessed, three-way, or outdoor fixtures. Additionally, there are CFLs especially for use with devices such as a dimmer, timer, or photoelectric eye. In some high-use areas, such as a foyer or bathroom, a CFL could wear out prematurely or experience excessive vibration or impact. For these trouble spots, check out Heavy Duty Rough Service bulbs from Feit Electric Company. Each bulb has a reinforced filament rated for 3,000 to 5,000 hours.

THE GREAT INDOORS

→ Small changes can have a huge impact on your bills—and the environment. A modest 20 percent reduction of energy use in U.S. homes could keep 558 billion pounds of CO_2 out of the atmosphere each year. And there are ways to save beyond the utility bills, too. From making your own non toxic cleaning supplies to fixing up the tool bench in the garage, here are a few small changes you can make, room by room.

RECYCLING BY THE NUMBERS

AMERICANS HAUL 82 MILLION TONS OF TRASH TO RECYCLING CENTERS EACH YEAR—JUST 32.5 PERCENT OF WHAT WE THROW OUT. HERE'S HOW MUCH ENERGY THAT RECYCLING ACTUALLY SAVES.

MATERIAL	RECYCLING RATE	ENERGY SAVED RECYCLING	CARBON EMISSIONS PREVENTED	PRICE PER TON	WORTH IT?
ALUMINUM (SODA CANS)	1,440,000 TONS DISCARDED/YEAR 45% IS RECYCLED	96%	10 TONS CO_2/ TON ALUMINUM	$1800-$2000	YES. EACH EMPTY CAN IS WORTH ABOUT 3 CENTS.
GLASS (BOTTLES AND JARS)	11,390,000 TONS DISCARDED/YEAR 25% IS RECYCLED	21%	0.34 TONS CO_2/ TON GLASS	$25-$40	MARGINAL SAVINGS. REUSE MAKES GREATER SENSE.
NEWSPRINT	12,360,000 TONS DISCARDED/YEAR 88% IS RECYCLED	45%	2.5 TONS CO_2/ TON NEWSPRINT	$90-$140	YES. DEMAND IS GREAT OVERSEAS.
SOFT-DRINK BOTTLES (PET, NO. 1)	940,000 TONS DISCARDED/YEAR 31% IS RECYCLED	76%	1.7 TONS CO_2/ TON PLASTIC	$360-$480	YES. PRICE HAS DOUBLED IN THE LAST FEW YEARS AND MARKET WILL CONTINUE TO MATURE.

Kitchen and Laundry

There's no room that guzzles energy quite like the kitchen. While you can't always replace an old fridge or washer and dryer set, try these inexpensive fixes to keep your energy and water use a bit more "green." From avoiding the purchase of precooked, prepackaged items to making your own detergent, here's our advice.

► WEEKEND PROJECT

TOOLS AND MATERIALS

- Plastic containers
- Power drill
- Window box
- Small pebbles
- Potting soil
- Plant seedlings

Cost: $40
Monthly Savings: $5
Payback: 8 months

PLANT A KITCHEN GARDEN

Find a sunny spot in your kitchen for a window box—inside. South-facing windows will get the most light. Begin with a simple herb garden, then consider branching out to small vegetables like cherry tomatoes. Basil, thyme, parsley, mint, and dill are easy to grow. With fresh food easily available, you will be more likely to cook at home.

1: Drill four small drainage holes in the bottom of each plastic container. Place a thin layer of pebbles in the bottom of each pot, then fill less than halfway with potting soil.

2: Plant the seedlings roots down, then fill the rest of the window box with soil to about 2in. below the lip of the container. Leave the stems of the seedlings uncovered.

3: Don't overwater. Soil should be slightly dry before watering. Use a self-watering bulb if necessary.

KNOW YOUR STUFF:
TERMITES STAY FOR DINNER

If you suspect a termite infestation in your home, you need to have a pest control contractor conduct a thorough inspection inside and outside the house to determine what to do. Termites can find their way through almost any kind of construction—concrete slabs included. They can enter through a crack as small as $1/64$ in., about equal to the diameter of the period at the end of this sentence. That's just enough space for one termite to squeeze through. Once inside, they will attack wood, the paper face on drywall, cellulose insulation, books, cardboard, leather, and even animal furs.

Your natural instincts are to protect your house and to take action as quickly as possible. This can cause you to make a snap decision that you may later regret. Although termites can cause serious damage, they work slowly, so you have time to do your homework, interview contractors, and come up with a plan. "When homeowners panic, they set themselves up for unscrupulous contractors of any type," says John Fasoldt, owner of United Exterminating in Cherry Hill, NJ.

The pest control inspection and treatment may require that carpet be taken up and baseboard trim removed (perhaps along with the drywall behind it) so that the base of the wall can be inspected.

There are several ways to treat for termites, though they're not all available in every area. The method you settle on will depend on local conditions and how the industry is regulated where you live. For that matter, the pest control company may suggest a combination of methods. Whatever the contractor suggests, your best bet is to be thoroughly informed about your options.

BAITING:

Baiting stations are implanted in the ground close to the house and in other areas termites are expected to be. This system's advantage is that it uses very little termiticide (in the bait) and does not require disruption to your home, such as drilling holes through the foundation slab. One disadvantage is that it works more slowly than other processes. Also, it's more expensive than other methods since it requires the stations to be monitored several times a year.

SOIL TREATMENT:

This involves drilling through concrete slabs and foundation walls outside the house, and sometimes inside, so that chemicals can be placed next to or under the foundation. The specifics of this treatment depend on how the house is built.

Soil treatment may involve using repellent or nonrepellent termiticide. Repellents kill but also repel termites. This treatment method depends on forming a continuous chemical barrier—sometimes a difficult proposition, depending on soil types and building characteristics.

Nonrepellent termiticides work differently. Termites can't detect the chemicals in the treated soil as they move through it. They then carry the termiticide back to the nest, where it kills other termites.

QUICK FIX

REPURPOSE ITEMS

Consider reusing or repurposing items before you toss them out. Explore new uses for the old junk like the ones we've listed below.

1: Bath and Dish Towels. Cut into smaller squares, an old bath towel can be used as a garage oil rag.

2: Broken Ceramic Dishes and Tile. If you have a rock tumbler, toss the pieces in. Use the gravel for a fish tank

or your herb garden. Alternatively, search for a local artist who would reuse the pieces in mosaic creation.

3: Glass Jars. Clean jars that held jelly and jam and use them to store loose nails, hooks, and screws.

QUICK FIX

COMMUNITY SUPPORTED AGRICULTURE (CSA)

If you want to eat high-quality, organic food cheaply—and don't want to grow it yourself—join a CSA. Visit LocalHarvest.org to sign up to receive a share of a local farmer's annual harvest. Not only will you receive a weekly basket of farm-fresh food, your help will keep a small farm operational.

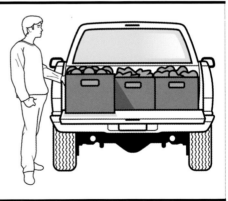

QUICK FIX

PEST CONTROL
Exterminators are expensive, and the chemicals they use are hazardous to your health and bad for the environment. Skip calling the exterminator and be your own pest control expert with a few do-it-yourself solutions.

1: Mice. Stuff copper wool into small mice openings. Mice will avoid it because they won't want to get their feet caught in the metal wool.

2: Cockroaches. Mix 1cup borax, 1cup flour, and 1cup sugar with water. The mixture can then be rolled into small balls. Put the balls on the floor, along the floorboards, spaced about 3 to 4 ft.

apart. After a week, sweep the balls up and throw them away, along with the newly deceased roaches.

3: Ants. These pests make their way inside through tiny crevices around window frames or doorways. Seal these hot spots with caulk. You can also try sprinkling borax or ground chili pepper around the problem areas.

4: Spiders. A word of warning: these pests love to eat insects, so if you get rid of them, you might end up with a bunch of unwanted bugs. The easiest way to rid your home of spiders is to vacuum them up, and be sure to vacuum their egg sacs, too. Spider egg sacs are usually fixed to a surface with a spider web, and they look a lot like cocoons.

TIPS OF THE TRADE:
CABINET DOOR FIX

If the laminate has come off the corners of your kitchen cabinet doors, take a careful look where it is peeling up. If the core of the door appears to be sound, then the repair is cosmetic and simple. Use a fine-tooth hacksaw blade or a putty knife to spread some moisture-resistant adhesive under the laminate. Then, use masking tape wrapped from the front of the door and around the edge to pull the laminate down. Remove the tape once the adhesive has set, and use a razor-sharp chisel to pare off globs of adhesive that squeeze out from under the laminate while they are still soft.

However, if moisture from cooking or cleaning has caused the core of the doors to crumble or otherwise fail, you're better off replacing those doors, or replacing all the doors in the kitchen. You will find it very difficult to make the laminate adhere properly to a deteriorated substrate. Turn to page 146 and get new (old) kitchen cabinets.

QUICK FIX

NO MORE BOTTLES
Over 8 billion gal. of bottled water were consumed in the United States in 2007, despite evidence that it's not necessarily safer than tap. Find out how your tap water compares by visiting the Environmental Working Group's Tap Water Quality Database (ewg.org/tapwater/yourwater). If you're still not satisfied, invest in a water filter or water purifier.

TOOLS AND MATERIALS

- 2 ft. of fine mesh screen
- Wire cutter scissors
- A dark felt pen

Cost: $10
Monthly Savings: $1
Payback: 10 months

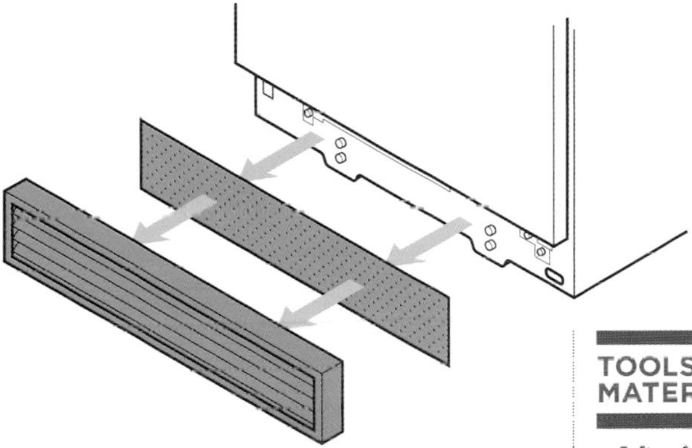

KITCHEN TLC

The condenser coils underneath the refrigerator are both a dispenser of heat and a magnet for dust—especially in homes with dirty kitchen floors or lots of pets. When they are dusty, your fridge will cycle on more frequently—and use more energy. Adding a screen to the refrigerator grille will help keep dirt and grime from getting swept up under the fridge and also keep the grille area clean of debris so that air flow is unrestricted. Keep further cleanings to a minimum by installing this screen.

1: Remove the grille from the bottom of the refrigerator.

2: Trace the perimeter of the grille with the pen and cut the pattern out of the mesh screen.

3: Push the screen into the backside of the grille and reattach the grille to the refrigerator.

4: Every few months, remove the grille, pull out the screen, and clean the screen with soap and water; allow the screen to dry, then reinsert it into the grille.

SAFE AND SOUND
RECOGNIZING TOXIC MOLD

Toxic black mold is a serious problem that can cause severe health problems and surface damage that can lead to expensive repairs. The first signs of mold are usually conditions that permit it to flourish. Kevin Roberts, president of the Mold Help Organization, points out that mold needs abundant moisture to grow, so if your part of the country experiences consistently high humidity, you need to be especially watchful. For the same reasons, he suggestions keeping an eye out for:

• Recurrent leaks in walls, which leave residual moisture

• Excessive condensation on pipes that run through confined areas with little air ventilation

• HVAC systems that experience severe fluctuations in temperature or humidity levels, or HVAC systems that leak

• A chronically leaky roof

• Flooding

If mold has made a home in yours, it's likely the first sign will be a telltale mildewy odor that doesn't go away. Other signs will be more blatant:

• Cracked or peeling paint on walls

QUICK FIX

OUT OF THE PAN
Use the smallest possible pot or pan when cooking on your stove top, and match it to the size of the burner's coils. When you use a pan that's too large or too small, energy is wasted and you risk burning the pan. According to the American Council for an Energy-Efficient Economy (ACEEE), a 6-in. pan on an 8-in. electric burner will waste over 40 percent of the heat produced.

- Buckling wall surfaces that are moist to the touch

- Discoloration (especially yellowing on darkening to black) or wall or ceiling surfaces

- Drywall tape coming loose

- Chronic and unexplained allergic symptoms in members of the household, with no apparent stimuli, or chronic sinus infections

- Visible mold growth on walls or ceilings

- Clogged vents or air ducts

- Cracked or disconnected hoses behind refrigerators from automatic ice makers/water dispensers or dishwashers

The first step to alleviating a mold problem is assessing its severity, which is often done best by a qualified testing company. Confined cases of mold can often be treated with removal of the affected nonporous area and use of simple treatments such as soap and water. Where the mold is pervasive—such as when it is growing throughout the home's HVAC system or inside of walls—you'll need to use a certified abatement professional. In addition to whatever action is taken to remove the mold, the conditions that caused it to appear in the first place must be remedied.

QUICK FIX

MINIMIZE THE COOKING AREA
There's no need to reheat just one plate in the oven. According to the ACEEE, a simple way to save energy is to match the cooking method to the meal. For example, while microwaves use a great deal of energy when operating, the cooking times are so drastically reduced that the energy use is just two-thirds of what a conventional oven would require for the same preparation. Find the correct balance of space heated to dish being prepared, or use an appliance designed for that particular type of meal, such as a crockpot or rice cooker.

GREEN AND CLEAN

Each time you spray a traditional cleaner, harmful chemicals are released into the air you breathe. The harsh additives can actually harm your furniture's surfaces, wearing away enamel and over time necessitating a replacement. But don't bother springing for the pricy eco-friendly cleaners when it's just as easy to make your own.

Cost: $20
Monthly Savings: $40
Payback: Immediate

1: Pots and Pans. Use a tablespoon of baking soda to scour your pots and pans. It's even better than commercial products because it won't leave scratches—or dull the surface.

2: Sinks, Tubs, Floors, and Countertops. A gentle but effective homemade cleaner can be made with 3 parts water, 1 part white vinegar, and a splash of lemon juice.

4: Drains. To eliminate unpleasant odors, pour a cup of white vinegar down the drain, let it stand for 30 minutes, then rinse with hot water. If you have a grease clog, try wrapping a heating pad around the drain trap until the metal becomes hot. This will melt the grease and allow you to flush it away with a running stream of hot water.

3: Carpet Stains. Sprinkle an oil stain with cornstarch, then wipe away with a wet cloth after absorption. For blood or wine stains, saturate with hydrogen peroxide and dab with a dry cloth.

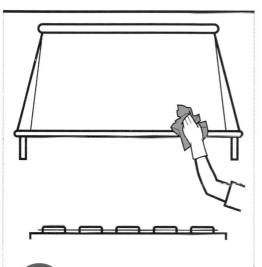

QUICK FIX

NONDISPOSABLE

Americans throw out 100 billion plastic bags each year, and with them 12 million barrels of oil that went into their manufacture. Paper bags, on the other hand, consume 14 million trees and are less efficient to transport. The answer? Avoid them and bring your own. Use the same solution for other "disposables" like canning jars and take-out food containers, which are reusable with just a simple washing.

QUICK FIX

CLEAN YOUR RANGE HOOD

There are three types of hood systems, each of which can develop blockages. The first is a simple metal filter system that catches particles drawn up through the hood's vacuum fan. These should be soaked in hot soapy water mixed with a half cup of ammonia (avoid the fumes and handle according to the directions on the bottle). If the filter is very greasy, replace it. Charcoal hood filters must be replaced if they are no longer filtering smoke out of the air. Some range hoods vent directly outside. If this type isn't cleaned out regularly, it won't ventilate, trapping heat and making your kitchen hotter than it needs to be. This will affect your air conditioning bill in the summer. Look for a blockage at the vent, especially in the screening that covers the damper (including any exterior blockage, such as a growth of ivy).

UPGRADE THE WASHER

When it's time to upgrade, make sure your washer meets Energy Star criteria, which will cut energy and water consumption by over 40 percent and save $550 in operating costs. While dryers are not currently monitored by Energy Star, simple steps such as using auto-dry or the automatic moisture sensor and cleaning the lint filter will keep your costs manageable.

QUICK
FIX

GREEN LAUNDRY

Each year, the average American household does about 400 loads of laundry. Reduce your costs—and your energy footprint—with these simple steps.

1: Wash the Right Amount.
Under-loading the washer risks throwing the drum off balance, which can break the machine beyond repair. If you overload, the washer won't take on adequate water because the weight-limit switch cannot tell the difference between clothing and water, and your clothes may require a second wash.

1 **2** 3 4 5 6

THE GREAT INDOORS

2: Check the Dryer's Manual. You can put more clothes in your dryer than you might think; double-check your manual for your model's specifics. If your dryer has a setting for auto-dry or an automatic moisture sensor, use it rather than the timer. This will avoid wasting energy and overdrying your clothes, which

can cause shrinkage, generate static electricity, and shorten the life of the fabric.

3: Use a Clothesline. Air-dry your clothes whenever possible. You'll use less energy, and your clothes will last longer. If you can't air-dry, save on drying time by drying similar fabrics together,

cleaning the lint filter after each use, and drying multiple loads in quick succession to take advantage of a preheated dryer.

4: Use Powder Detergent. The only difference between liquid and powder detergent is the addition of water—and the extra cost of transportation and energy.

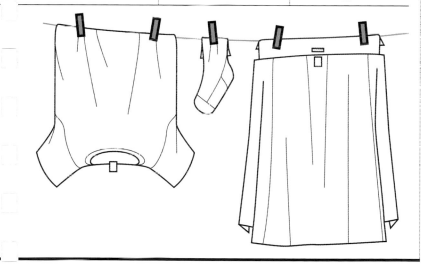

Bathroom

 One of the most often-used rooms in the house, your bathroom consumes energy to do everything from heating the bathwater to flushing the toilet. Taking just a few green steps will help to prolong the lifespan of your bathtub, toilet, and even your shower curtain.

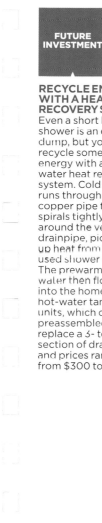

FUTURE INVESTMENT

RECYCLE ENERGY WITH A HEAT RECOVERY SYSTEM

Even a short hot shower is an energy dump, but you can recycle some of the energy with a drain-water heat recovery system. Cold water runs through a copper pipe that spirals tightly around the vertical drainpipe, picking up heat from the used shower water. The prewarmed water then flows into the home's hot-water tank. The units, which come preassembled, replace a 3- to 5-ft. section of drainpipe, and prices range from $300 to $500.

QUICK FIX

SHAKE IT OUT

Shake the excess water from the shower curtain into the tub after every shower to reduce moisture that encourages mold and damages your walls and ceiling. Once a month, wipe down the curtain with 1 part vinegar, 4 parts water solution to kill mold and bacteria and keep hard water spotting at bay.

TIPS OF THE TRADE:
PATCHING HOLES IN DRYWALL

If you're ready to give a room a low-budget makeover with a coat of paint, remember that the preparation should actually take longer than the painting itself. To end up with a paint job worthy of your time, first clean the walls thoroughly with soap and water. Rinse with clean water before beginning.

Patch nail and screw holes. Patching compound works great if you use this easy technique. Many times, when you take out an old nail or screw, it takes part of the wall covering with it, leaving it torn and sticking out. Often, those torn fibers won't lie down flat, no matter how carefully you apply patching compound. Try this quick solution: place the head of a carriage bolt over the hole and tap it with a hammer. The round head of the bolt will create a smooth dimple in the surface. The hole vanishes once you fill in the surface.

Small-hole patching. Putty, spackling paste, or drywall compound can all work for small holes. For slightly larger holes, you should use mesh tape or a convenient drywall patch. These patches are usually thin squares of metal covered with self-adhesive mesh tape. Just peel off the packing and place it over the hole; then, to hide the patch, apply a thin layer of joint compound.

Large-hole patching. To patch a drywall hole bigger than an inch, you will need to replace a section of the drywall with a patch. The easiest way to do this is with a drywall repair kit that has special repair clips to attach the new patch to the wall. The clips support the new patch and then "disappear." A smooth, clean wall is the result.

First, remove the damaged area with a drywall saw. You can also use a utility knife to make a series of cuts. Cut out a section in a square or rectangular shape. Next, slip the drywall repair clips onto the edges of the damaged wall. Using the screws provided in the kit, screw the clips into place. Then, cut a patch from a scrap of drywall that matches the hole you cut. Simply attach the patch to the drywall clips by driving screws through the patch and into the clips. The exposed clips will snap off, and you can cover the patch seams with mesh tape and joint compound.

Hide wall stains. Once you've patched any holes, you need to hide any stains; otherwise, they may bleed through your new paint coat. A few coats of stain blocker does a great job hiding and sealing stains. Look for eco-friendly transitional primers that are formaldehyde free and Leadership Energy and Environmental Design certified, such as AFM SafeCoat.

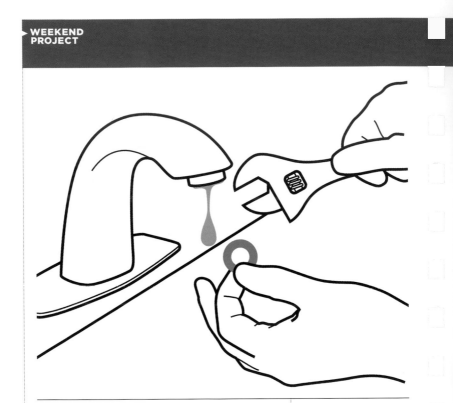

FIX A LEAKY FAUCET

A faucet dripping once per second does more than shred REM sleep: it wastes up to 3,000 gal. per year. Reduce your indoor water usage by up to 20 gal. per day by fixing the leaks. While most can be repaired by replacing a washer, a cartridge faucet is slightly more complex—bring along the old cartridge when buying a new one.

1: Regardless of the faucet, begin the repair by turning off the shutoff valve on the supply line to the sink. This is located under the sink or in the basement.

2: Next, close the sink drain to avoid losing small parts; then disassemble the faucet. Take note of the order of the parts to aid in reassembly. To ensure an exact match, bring the removed components to the hardware store or home center. When repairing a pair of compression faucets, repair one faucet at a time to avoid mixing the parts and causing the faucet handles to open and shut opposite their correct counterclockwise and clockwise operation.

TOOLS AND MATERIALS

- Plumber's wrench
- 1 cup vinegar
- Rag
- Dish detergent
- Heatproof plumber's grease
- Drain plug

3: Clean mineral-encrusted parts (that will not be replaced with new parts) with warm vinegar before reinstalling them. If friction makes the O-rings tough to install, use a drop or two of liquid dish detergent to lubricate the parts.

4: Hot water wears out washers more quickly than cold water, so the washer on a hot faucet usually wears out before the washer on a cold faucet. Protect the washer with heatproof plumber's grease.

Cost: $1
Monthly Savings: $0.35
Payback: 3 months

FAUCET UPDATE
Check the flow rate of faucets with flow bags, which are available in water audit kits provided by many water utilities. It should be less than 2.2 gal. per minute (gpm) in the kitchen and 1.5 gpm in the bathroom. If it's time to upgrade, look for faucets with the EPA's new WaterSense label.

**FUTURE
INVESTMENT**

INSTALL A WATER-EFFICIENT TOILET

If your toilet was installed pre-1983, it may use 5-gal. of water or more for every flush. Check for a sticker with a date stamp inside the tank. Today's water-efficient models are designed to use 1.6 gal. or less per flush. Some local utilities offer rebates of $50 to $100 if a high-flow toilet is replaced with a low-flow; make sure to check if you are eligible.

▶ **WEEKEND
PROJECT**

BE YOUR OWN PLUMBER

Your home center's plumbing aisle can be totally confusing and bathroom projects can just be downright grimy. Here's how to fix those creaks and drips without breaking a sweat.

1: Drip, Take 2

There's still hope if, after making a repair to a compression faucet or valve, you get a small drip around its handle stem. Wind a little graphite or Teflon stem packing material around the stem. It's probably best to buy the material before beginning the repair—it's only a couple of bucks, and chances are you're going to need it.

2: Yellow Tape

If you're installing or replacing a gas kitchen range, use the Teflon tape that comes in the yellow container, not the blue—it's designed for lubricating and sealing water connections, not gas.

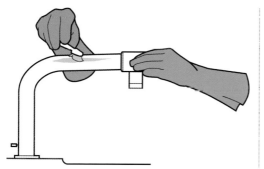

3: Double Scrub
Keep an old toothbrush in your plumbing tool kit. It's good for gently removing dirt and mineral deposits.

4: Valve-o-Clean
Use warm vinegar or Calcium Lime Rust (CLR) cleaner to remove stubborn mineral deposits from valves and faucets, plus parts that you're not going to replace. Many old parts can be kept in service if they are cleaned.

5: Friendly Grease
When you reinstall a freshly cleaned and repaired faucet stem, apply a tiny dab of plumber's grease on the washer for the hot-water faucet. Washers on the hot-water side of a two-handle faucet wear out more quickly than those on the cold-water side. The grease provides a little protection and helps them last longer.

6: Smart Start
Keep a screw pitch gauge in your toolbox. It helps identify the thread characteristics of parts that need to be replaced. For example, faucet aerators come with different threads, and knowing what you are replacing will save you multiple trips to the hardware store.

7: Rag and Round
When your tubing cutter starts to get dull, buy a replacement cutting wheel for it rather than chucking the entire tool. A dull wheel will cause the cutter to leave a ragged edge— or you'll need to apply excessive force when making the cut. This force will bend the tubing out of round, making it difficult to place a fitting over it.

8: Prime Time
Always be sure to apply primer to PVC pipe before cementing it to a fitting. It's code required, and it's unlikely that you'll get a watertight joint without it. The primer is dyed purple so that a plumbing inspector or other code official will see that it has been applied.

DO-OVER

Stained and cracked caulk can be altogether unsightly. It's very easy and inexpensive to remove and recaulk. Not only will your bathroom look better, but you'll remove mold build up and keep the water where it should be—in the bathtub.

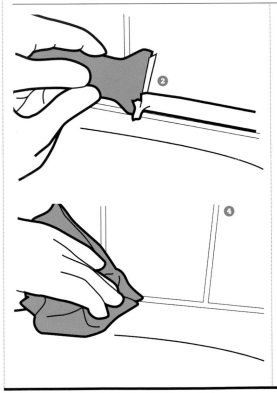

1: Soften the caulk by applying caulk remover.

2. Slice through the softened caulk using a utility knife with a fresh blade. If you're lucky, most of it will fall free. On the other hand, if there are several layers or if the caulk is very thick, you may need to pull the material from the joint with a pair of needle-nose pliers.

3. Rake remaining chunks of caulk from the joint using the hook end of a painter's five-in-one tool.

4. Now, clean the surface and remove mildew. Use a nonammoniated bath cleaner to remove soap scum. If you do decide to use bleach, do not use an ammoniated cleaner

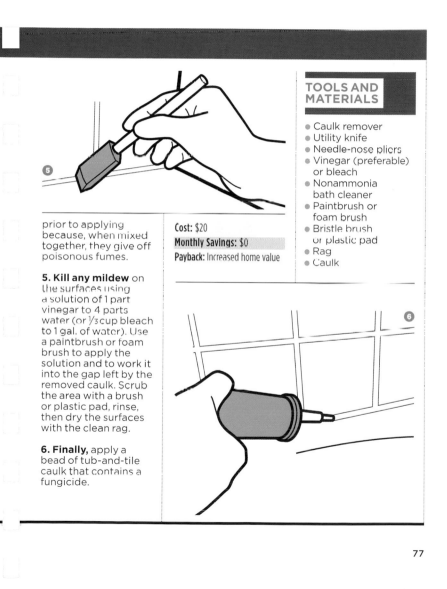

TOOLS AND MATERIALS

- Caulk remover
- Utility knife
- Needle-nose pliers
- Vinegar (preferable) or bleach
- Nonammonia bath cleaner
- Paintbrush or foam brush
- Bristle brush or plastic pad
- Rag
- Caulk

prior to applying because, when mixed together, they give off poisonous fumes.

5. Kill any mildew on the surfaces using a solution of 1 part vinegar to 4 parts water (or ⅓ cup bleach to 1 gal. of water). Use a paintbrush or foam brush to apply the solution and to work it into the gap left by the removed caulk. Scrub the area with a brush or plastic pad, rinse, then dry the surfaces with the clean rag.

6. Finally, apply a bead of tub-and-tile caulk that contains a fungicide.

Cost: $20
Monthly Savings: $0
Payback: Increased home value

Living Room
and Bedrooms

Most time at home is either spent in the living room or bedroom. In this section you'll find suggestions to raise your indoor quality of life. Here's a quick tip: even if your house is properly insulated, the air quality may be poor. Culprits include furniture with particle board, PVC (on carpet backing), and VOCs (volatile organic compounds) such as formaldehyde and benzene. What can you do about it? Just opening a window can help break down the CO_2.

QUICK FIX

FRESHEN UP
Skip the commercial air fresheners; most contain chemicals that aren't so fresh. Make your own solution instead and you'll breathe easier. Simply add a tablespoon of essential oil (eucalyptus suggested) to a 12 oz. mister bottle full of water, shake lightly, and spray into the air.

QUICK FIX

ADD THE CURTAINS
Window treatments, whether blinds or curtains, are your best defense against cold winter drafts and the hot summer sun. A quick installation may be performed using two 2-in. wooden blocks and some heavy-duty glue. Simply nail the curtain rod hardware to the block, mount the block to the wall using the glue, and wait for it to dry.

MOTH-OLOGY

Use natural cedar chips in closets and drawers to ward off moths. Place the chips in a plastic food container with slits cut into the lid. Periodically refresh the container with new chips. Another option for keeping moths at bay is to take old bars of soap, put them in a Ziploc bag, and smash the soap into small pieces. Poke a few holes in the bag and the soap smell will keep moths out of your closet.

QUICK
FIX

VACUUM IN THE UPRIGHT POSITION

Choose an upright vacuum cleaner. They have more suction power—and thus more bang for the buck. Save energy and get your floors, carpets, and rugs clean in less time.

SAFE AND SOUND:
LEAD PAINT REMOVAL

There is no economical or efficient way to remove lead-based paint. Repainting with an oil-based paint will not solve the problem because the lead will eventually leach through the top coat. There are currently three acceptable methods of abating lead paint:

- Replacement

- Removal

- Encapsulating or covering

Replacement is the most appropriate for windows, sills, woodwork, and doors, but not for exterior siding. Removal of the lead-based paint, which includes scraping the surfaces using hand scrapers, chemical solvents, or heat guns, is the most costly because it is labor intensive and generates large amounts of lead dust, which must then be disposed of in special landfills.

The least costly approach is encapsulating and covering. The exterior walls may be covered with aluminum siding, which can be made from recycled materials and is extremely eco-friendly. However, the walls should first be treated with an encapsulant to prevent lead-based paint contamination during the siding installation. The encapsulant is sprayed or rolled on. It bonds chemically with the lead paint below to prevent it from leaching.

If exterior lead-based paint is peeling and flaking, it's likely the ground around the building is contaminated from lead dust and flakes. If the soil is contaminated, it should be covered with sod or gravel.

Before any work is undertaken, engage the services of a trained lead-paint inspector to determine the extent of the problem.

TIPS OF THE TRADE:
HOW TO PAINT

The goal of every painter is to paint neatly and quickly. This can be challenging. Fortunately, there are dozens of tricks, shortcuts, and trade secrets specifically for painting—many more than for any other home-improvement activity. Try one or all of the following techniques and I'm sure you'll end up with a paint job nice enough to show off to the neighbors.

TINT THE PRIMER:
Whether you're painting interior walls or exterior siding, a coat of primer is key to obtaining professional-looking results. Primer serves three main functions: it blocks stains and resinous knots from bleeding through, it provides one-coat coverage for the paint top coat and most importantly, it improves adhesion, which greatly reduces blisters and extends the life of the top coat.

To further enhance the coverage of the top coat, try this pro tip: tint the primer toward the finished color by mixing a small amount of top coat paint into the primer. (Be sure the primer and top coat are both latex based or both oil based; never mix coatings with dissimilar solutions.) This will greatly enhance the ability of the top coat to hide the prepped surface completely, especially when painting a lighter top coat over an existing darker color.

INVEST IN CANVAS:
Canvas drop cloths are durable, and rip and puncture resistant. They lay flat as you walk across them, presenting less of a tripping hazard; seldom, if ever, must you tape canvas to the floor. Canvas also absorbs paint drips, unlike plastic drop cloths, which become slippery when spattered with

wet paint. You're much less likely to pick up paint on your shoe soles from canvas. Canvas drop cloths can easily be folded around corners and doorways—something that's virtually impossible to do with plastic sheeting. Plus, canvas can be reused countless times, which makes using them eco-friendly when compared with discarding yards of plastic drop cloths after just one use.

ROLL WITH A POLE:

When painting rooms, forget the ladder and get a telescoping extension pole for your paint roller. Extension poles come in various sizes, but one that extends from about 18 in. to 30 or 36 in. offers plenty of reach for painting rooms with ceilings that are 9 ft. or lower. There are also extra-long extension poles that telescope up to about 18 ft. for painting cathedral ceilings and loft spaces.

Look for an extension pole with a soft, nonslip rubber grip and a rigid metal core. And be sure the threaded end of the pole is metal, too. All-plastic handles are too flexible, making them hard to control, and the plastic gets fatigued over time and can snap under pressure. Also check to be sure the telescoping shaft locks securely in position and doesn't collapse when forced.

RECORD THE COLOR:

Keep track of the brand name and color of the paint used so you can buy more when it comes time to touch up or repaint the room. Instead of attempting to record this information in a notebook, write the vital information (brand name, paint color, paint number) on a piece of masking tape and stick it to the back of a light-switch plate before replacing it on the wall. It'll stay there until it's time to repaint.

DIM AND DIMMER

Modern electronic dimmers save energy by switching the light on and off 120 times per second, which reduces the energy moving through the circuit. Buy the best quality dimmer switch that you can find; these switches are more durable and energy efficient than inexpensive dimmers. You will need to match the dimmer's wattage rating to the load as well as to the type of load, such as incandescent or low-voltage lighting. Don't use a dimmer to control a ceiling fan. And never use a dimmer to control power to an outlet or on a circuit with a shared neutral (the grounded conductor).

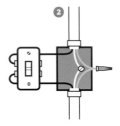

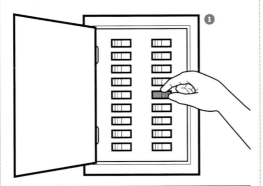

the wire stripper to strip off about 3/8-in. of the insulation. If needed, strip the wires that are attached to the new dimmer switch.

5: Connect one of the black wires in the electrical box to one from the dimmer switch by placing the bare wires next to each other. Then twist on a wire nut connector. The bare wires should be completely covered by the connector. Do the same for the other set of wires. Connect all the ground wires also.

6: Tuck the wires back into the box in a zigzag pattern, and push the

1: Turn off the circuit at the main service panel.

2: Use a screwdriver to remove the switch plate, and then the old switch, saving the screws.

3: Disconnect the wires that connect to the old switch.

4: Use the wire cutters to cut off the bare wire just below the insulation, then use

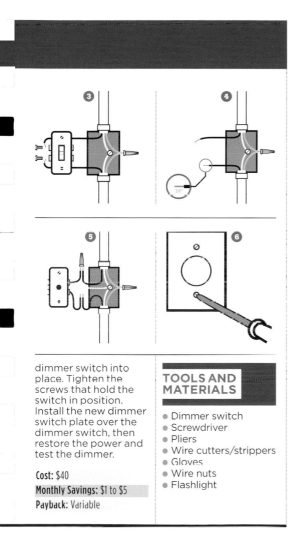

INVEST IN SOLAR SCREENS

Indoor window solar screens are made of a polyester mesh, which allows for good visibility. The screens block sun glare and almost all solar heat—effectively reducing indoor temperatures by as much as 25 degrees. Self-installation is possible with a DIY kit from the manufacturer. For the winter months, consider vinyl screens, which keep the cold air out while allowing the solar heat to warm the indoors.

dimmer switch into place. Tighten the screws that hold the switch in position. Install the new dimmer switch plate over the dimmer switch, then restore the power and test the dimmer.

Cost: $40
Monthly Savings: $1 to $5
Payback: Variable

TOOLS AND MATERIALS

- Dimmer switch
- Screwdriver
- Pliers
- Wire cutters/strippers
- Gloves
- Wire nuts
- Flashlight

SAFE AND SOUND:
ASBESTOS REMOVAL

If your older house has a spray-on "popcorn" ceiling, its coating may contain asbestos. The only sure way to know is to have a sample analyzed by a testing laboratory. If it does contain asbestos, don't panic: the simple presence of asbestos is not a health hazard. If the material is in good condition and is unlikely to be disturbed, then any effects of the asbestos are considered negligible.

If your ceiling contains asbestos and you have deteriorated or damaged sections, asbestos fibers may be released into the air, creating a health hazard. In this case, contact an asbestos abatement company and have the ceiling removed.

Do not simply scrape the "popcorn" off because you'll be releasing asbestos fibers into the air. Contact your local health department or the Environmental Protection Agency for the names of licensed abatement companies.

FUTURE INVESTMENT

RIP OUT
CARPETING
Carpeting can hide many creatures like dust mites and fleas. Make the switch to hardwood or cork floors to improve the quality of the air in your bedroom. Don't just toss the carpet once you're done: Visit the Web site of the Carpet America Recovery Effort (CARE) to learn how to recycle it in your area. (carpetrecovery.org)

QUICK FIX

TAKE OFF YOUR SHOES
Wear slippers indoors. Just by removing your shoes, you can significantly reduce the amount of outdoor pollutants indoors—from pollen to bacteria, mold, and viruses.

Basement and Garage

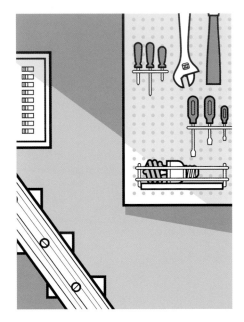

Your basement and garage can be the catchall rooms for the things you probably don't need but maybe just can't find a way to get rid of: old furniture, broken toys, lamps with faulty wiring. Take the time to organize to reduce waste, get rid of old stuff, and put the remainder to good use. A thorough purging of the clutter might just give you the space—and the incentive—to finish those projects on your workbench. Turn your basement and garage into productive living spaces with these tips.

► **WEEKEND PROJECT**

GET A FURNACE TUNE-UP

A $100 to $200 annual tune-up can help reduce your heating costs instantly. Systems that are not properly maintained may be 50 percent less efficient, and annual tune-ups allow you to fix any problems before they cost you thousands. It's best to have a licensed professional do the necessary work. Find a home heating (HVAC) contractor in the Yellow Pages.

1: During your tune-up, the contractor will inspect the flue and blower. Your furnace will be inspected for rust, missing bolts, and so on, and the burners will be cleaned. The carbon monoxide levels will be checked. You will get an indication of your fuel usage and if the furnace's performance can be improved.

2: Make sure that a record is made of the furnace's inspection; this is important for your homeowners insurance, and also if the house is being prepped for sale.

Cost: $100 to $200
Monthly Savings: Up to $40
Payback: 6 months

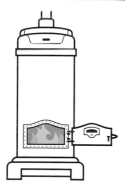

FUTURE INVESTMENT

GET A NEW FURNACE

Consider replacing an old furnace. Outdated units can be big energy wasters. When shopping for a new unit don't just compare the installed price per BTU (British thermal unit). Calculate the life-cycle costs of comparable units with different EERs (Energy Efficiency Ratios). The best time to switch fuels is when replacing the furnace. No matter what you decide, replacing a furnace is a time you will call in the pros. Often, the purchase and the installation of the new furnace will be a package deal.

SAFE AND SOUND:
HOW TO DISPOSE OF HAZARDOUS WASTE

It's time to clean out your garage. But the hazardous waste can't just go out on your curb on trash day. Did you know that there are around 750 million gal. of used motor oil recycled in this country every year, and it takes only 1 gal. of improperly disposed oil to contaminate 1 million gal. of groundwater?

Recycling law and practice vary considerably among township, county, and state jurisdictions. You should be able to get details about recycling practice from the department of public works at your city hall or county seat, or its Web site. Some kinds of items, like paint, may be picked up on special days from the curbside. Some counties make it more difficult. You'll have to do some leg work to find out what your options are. Here's our advice about what to do with what's left over when you work on your car, truck, or motorcycle at home.

USED OIL AND FILTERS
We recommend getting an oil drain pan, available for a few dollars. It holds 10 quarts, enough for a couple of oil changes, has a tightfitting lid to keep the oil contained, and a grate to hold the filter to allow it to drain completely. Commercial shops are required to crush or puncture the used filters to facilitate draining. When it's time, decant the used oil into clean, dry plastic bottles (empty milk jugs are perfect) and label them as used engine oil. In most states, any shop that does oil changes is required to take modest quantities of used oil from consumers. The used oil is either recycled back into other petroleum products or burned in special furnaces for heat.

If you do buy your motor oil in quarts, remember to drain the last few drops of oil out of each plastic quart bottle. An hour of draining upside down, multiplied by the residue of 4 other quarts (one oil change's worth), is often a couple of fingers of oil. Save this for your oil can or for topping off the lawnmower. Now the empty plastic bottles can be tossed into the recycling with the household plastics, without contaminating the entire recycling infrastructure with oil.

COOLANT

Drain the radiator into a pan, with as little spillage as possible. Fill the system with water and run it until the engine warms up enough to open the thermostat, and then for a few minutes longer to mix thoroughly. Drain, fill, and drain again. This double flush will purge 99 percent of the old coolant. Now you can refill with the correct amount of fresh coolant and top off with water.

What to do with the old coolant? Many larger shops have coolant recycling machines. These actually distill the glycol out of the old coolant, and the shop can add an additive package and reuse it as if it were new. The water boils off and all that's left is a few teaspoonfuls of sludge. Call around to find one of these machines; the shop will probably let you drop off your old coolant. But there's one very important caveat: use a clean drain pan and funnel, and clean containers to ferry the coolant. If you use the same drain pan for oil or other solvents and even a few drops of oil wind up in the coolant, it can't be recycled.

PAINT AND GASOLINE

Most automotive paint used in the aftermarket is solvent based—either enamel or lacquer. (A lot of new cars are painted at the factory with waterborne paint systems.) And many municipalities won't take this type of paint or its companion thinners as waste. If you have a secure, well-ventilated place, one that isn't likely to start a fire or poison children or pets, you can do what we usually do for small quantities of leftover or

(cont.) SAFE AND SOUND:
HOW TO DISPOSE OF
HAZARDOUS WASTE

contaminated paint thinner and gasoline—just leave the can open in a safe, warm place until it dries completely. (Don't try this with coolant —it takes far too long to dry out.) Larger quantities should go into the hazardous waste system. The gasoline additive MTBE is turning into a major issue as a groundwater contaminant.

BRAKE FLUID

Brake fluid is alcohol based. It's toxic when ingested. When bleeding brakes, catch the runoff in a jar. Brake fluid from a jar that's been opened for more than a few months probably has absorbed enough water to reduce its boiling point past the point of safety. To dispose of new or unused brake fluid, pour it into a container of cat litter. The brake fluid will evaporate within a few days. As with paint, keep this away from pets and children, and any source of ignition.

BATTERIES

The toxic lead in car batteries can contaminate groundwater. Fortunately, batteries are recyclable. Both the sulfuric acid and the lead plates are reusable after only a modest amount of processing. In most states, when you buy a new battery, the vendor will charge you a small fee that's refunded when you return your old battery. And most of these shops will take in old batteries. If not, the city or county will have a place to drop them off, so there's no need to dispose of them illegally.

TIRES

Some areas recycle tires by using them as supplementary fuel in cement kilns. The very high temperatures required to drive the water out of limestone and transform it into portland cement also ensure the complete combustion of the rubber and fabric in tires. A side benefit is the molten steel that collects in the bottom of the firebox. Most shops that sell tires have a way to dispose of old tires, although they may charge a modest fee. Some municipalities will take a few tires from a homeowner, either on regular trash day or at a special time or place.

SAFE AND SOUND:
RADON VENTILATION

Radon is a colorless, odorless gas that occurs from the decay of radium, a metallic, radioactive element. The degree of threat it poses to your health is a matter of some controversy, as its dangers have been extrapolated from the health statistics of uranium miners, specifically focusing on the occurrences of lung cancer. As the Environmental Protection Agency considers radon to be a threat, selling your home could be difficult if your radon levels are high and a radon removal system is not installed.

Take radon mitigation measures when a short-term test measurement is higher than 20 picocuries per liter of air (pCi/L). An effective method of reducing that level is to install a system that uses fans and piping to reduce the radon from beneath a house's basement slab. Holes are bored in the house's basement slab, pipes are inserted into the holes and sealed to the slab, and an inline fan pulls the gas from below the slab and exhausts it out through a roof vent.

In cases in which the radon reading is less than 20 pCi/L, a long-term test is recommended to determine the radon level more accurately. A long-term test spans one heating season and lasts anywhere from 3 to 12 months. If the long term test shows a level of 4 pCi/L or higher, it's common practice to install a radon ventilation system like the one discussed earlier.

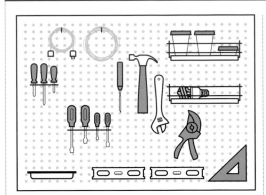

CUSTOMIZE YOUR PEG BOARD WALL ORGANIZER

There's just something about the way it makes tools stand crisply at attention, ready for their next assignment. Still, pegboard's shortcomings are well-known. Eventually holes can elongate, causing tools to slip off. And hooks and clips don't always suit what you want to hang. Before you toss your organizer and it ends up in a landfill, try your hand at making these quick, custom tool hangers.

1: Big hammers, like ball-peen and framing tools, are tough to hang because of the head shapes. Cut two pieces of 1-in. aluminum flat stock to length and bend them into L's. Fasten each L to the board with hexhead sheetmetal screws (5/16 x 3/4, or No. 12 or 14 for pegboard with smaller perforations). Offset each L to suit the hammer head.

2: If your screwdriver rack is loose, remove the rack and install threaded inserts (1/4-20) into the stripped-out pegboard holes. Now take a piece of 1-in.-sq. perforated steel tubing, cut it to length and cut away the face of the tubing at the ends to make mounting flanges. If needed, enlarge holes in the tubing to fit the screwdriver tips.

3: To get your long, thin tools to hang neatly, make a rack from aluminum L stock to suit the tools' sizes and shapes. Cut small slots in the face of the L using a hacksaw, then smooth each slot with a Dremel tool that has a grindstone chucked in it. Size and space each slot to accommodate

the tool's shaft and to leave adequate space between each handle.

4: Create a grab-and-go section to allow fast and easy access to the tools you use the most. Estimate the size of the rack you need, then use a hacksaw to cut mild-steel rod (1/8-in. dia.) to length; allow a little extra. Here's your work sequence: Bend the first mounting hook to shape with pliers; bend the

rack to shape; bend the second mounting hook; cut off the excess rod.

Difficulty: Amateur

Cost: About $45

Pay-Off: Save on replacement costs

TOOLS AND MATERIALS

- Safety glasses
- Power drill
- Hacksaw
- Pliers
- Dremel tool
- 1-in. Aluminum flat stock
- 10-30 hexhead sheet metal screws
- 1-in.-sq. perforated steel tubing
- 1-2 ft. diameter mild-steel rod (⅛-in. dia.)

CHANGE THE FURNACE FILTER

Clean or change your furnace filter at least once per month during heating season. A dirty filter will result in an inefficient furnace and poor air quality.

1: Turn off the furnace or set the thermostat to its lowest setting.	**2: Locate the filter access panel,** usually on the lower front or along the side.	**3: Gently pop open** or pull down the panel door; tools usually aren't needed.

4: Locate the filter—a framed mesh rectangular screen that is usually near the blower. Slide it out.

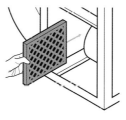

5: If you don't already have a new filter on hand, measure the filter and take the dimensions with you to the hardware store to purchase a new one.

6: If the filter is reusable, take it into the backyard and carefully hose off the dust particles, or vacuum it clean with a shop vacuum.

7: Make sure the filter is dry before replacing it—a wet filter will collect dirt quickly.

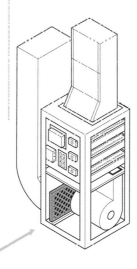

QUICK FIX

RIM JOIST SEAL
Heat can billow out from the boundary where the frame of your house sits on the foundation. From inside the basement, use caulking or spray foam (if the gap is bigger than Ð-in.) along the top and bottom of the rim joist to plug leaks. Then add rigid foam insulation or fiberglass batts, cut to fit, around the entire perimeter.

QUICK FIX

INSTALL A DEHUMIDIFIER
If you're having problems with moisture and surface condensation in your basement, consider installing a dehumidifier to combat the mold and rot. Opt for a small model and the waste heat it will give off won't be overwhelming in the summer.

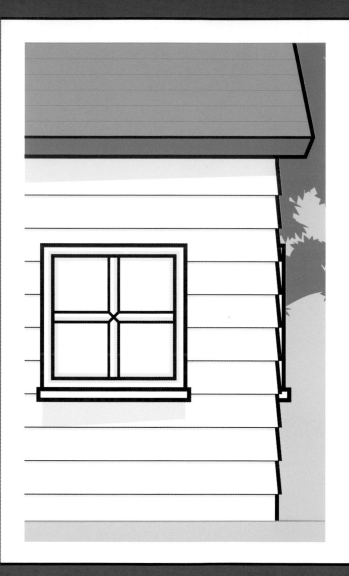

THE EXTERIOR OF YOUR HOME

→ The elements play havoc with any exterior part of your home, from the garage door to the walkway—and then there's the fact that yards and gardens tend to attract more than their fair share of visitors with destructive tendencies. Replacing gutters, fixing a leaky roof, and other maintenance can be costly, but taking care of the little problems will save you a bundle. This chapter will show you how to add value to your home, reduce energy costs, and expand your outdoor living space.

TIPS OF THE TRADE
WHEN TO WATER YOUR GRASS

NOT ALL LAWNS ARE CREATED EQUAL. BEFORE YOU DRAG OUT YOUR SPRINKLER SYSTEM, CONSIDER THESE FACTORS, ALL OF WHICH WILL AFFECT HOW FREQUENTLY YOUR LAWN NEEDS WATER:

Species of grass. Consider planting these water-thrifty alternatives to classic Kentucky bluegrass, which takes a lot of water and chemicals to keep it healthy in drier, hotter parts of the country. In variable climates: Western fescue (*Festuca occidentalis*), crested wheat grass (*Agropyron cristatum*). In hot climates: Blue grama (*Bouteloua gracilis*), buffalo grass (*Buchloe dactyloides*).

Type of soil. If you have sandy soil instead of loamy, your watering demands will be more frequent.

Rainfall. You don't need to pay a water bill for this natural resource.

Slope. If you're on a hill, the water may be running off faster than it's seeping in. Try watering in 15 to 20 minute intervals to give water time to filter into the soil.

Depth of soil. Use a pitchfork or shovel to find out what is located under your turf. If you have a solid layer of bedrock 2 in. down, your grass root system will not be holding much water and you will need to water more frequently— but less at a time.

Roofing and Siding

Maintaining the integrity of your house's structure requires going beyond painting and power washing and is the first line of defense against cooling and heating bills. Eco-friendly siding options have become even more affordable and durable. Green roofs, complete with vegetation, now appear on the sloped roofs of single-family homes, and other alternatives such as aluminum roofs (which reflect the sun's heat rather than absorbing it) have become widely available. The Cool Roof Rating Council (CRRC) provides a comparison of roofing materials and their eco-rating on its Web site. (coolroofs.org)

FUTURE INVESTMENT

INSTALL LOW-VOLTAGE OUTDOOR LIGHTING

If you plan to illuminate your driveway or garage, make sure you invest in an Energy Star– approved low-voltage component kit. Kits come with the transformer size, the length and size of the wire, and the number of allowable fixtures all figured out for you. For greater savings, build your own, but be aware: contrary to popular opinion, low-voltage systems can start fires when overextended. Too many fixtures or too long a run can cause low-voltage wires to overheat. If you plan to design your own system, make sure you use a transformer with a built-in breaker.

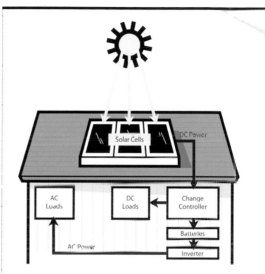

FUTURE INVESTMENT

SOLAR ENERGY

A number of different sun-powered technologies are finally approaching maturity as scalable and cost-effective options. Photovoltaic (PV) technology converts sunlight directly into electricity for household use. Companies like First Solar (firstsolar.com) have succeeded in bringing second-generation, silicon-free solar panels to the market at half the cost of traditional silicon panels. A solar power system can cost upward of $8,000 and has drawbacks (it's best on shade-free, sloped, and south-facing roofs; storing energy may require being connected to the utility grid; and electrical codes can be a hassle), but harnessing the sun has finally become reality. Consult with an expert when choosing your optimal system.

TIPS OF THE TRADE:
QUICK FIXES FOR EASY MISTAKES

The goal was so clear, the steps so logical. Then somehow, suddenly, something went wrong. For even the handiest, the road to DIY failure can be paved with good intentions. If you've ever turned a hacksaw blade into a projectile, corroded the brakes on a car, or caused a computer to self-destruct, read on.

STIRRED, NOT SHAKEN

Your bright idea: Paint stores use an agitator to mix paints, blending the pigment, binder, and solvent. You follow their lead and shake a can of varnish.

The dismal result: Shaking varnish or polyurethane creates thousands of tiny bubbles that will be visible when it dries, says Chris Harding, technical director for Waterlox Coatings. Paint gets bubbles, too, but has silicone and mineral oil that burst them by reducing surface tension. The action of rolling and brushing the paint bursts the rest by pushing millions of tiny, but sharp, color pigments against them.

Next time around: Stir your varnish thoroughly, but gently, with a clean paint stick. Save the shaking for the paint (and certain mixed drinks).

FENCED IN A CORNER

Your bright idea: You want your new fence to last, so you build it with pressure-treated posts cut to length.

The dismal result: The cut exposes wood cells not saturated with chemical preservatives, which protect pressure-treated lumber against damage from insects and fungi. You just provided an entry point for the rot you were trying to avoid.

Next time around: Go ahead and cut, but dip the end in preservative or apply it with a brush. Use a product that contains copper naphthenate, such as Cuprinol.

CREEPING CORROSION

Your bright idea: Because steel nails rust, you use an aluminum roofing nail to secure a loose piece of copper step flashing where roof and sidewall meet.

The dismal result: When two dissimilar metals are brought together in moist conditions, one rapidly corrodes (the anode—in this case, the nail) while the other does not (the cathode, or flashing). The problem, known as galvanic corrosion, is made worse because the cathode is significantly larger than the anode, a phenomenon called area effect.

Next time around: If you must put a nail through flashing, use an aluminum nail on aluminum flashing and a copper nail on copper flashing. Copper nails are expensive, but not nearly as costly as replacing the flashing.

SMOOTH MOVE

Your bright idea: You pour new concrete to replace a cracked pad, choosing a hot, sunny day.

The dismal result: "If you don't cure concrete properly," says Terry Collins, an engineer with the Portland Cement Association, "it won't reach maximum strength." Your new pad fractures.

Next time around: Collins recommends placing a wet blanket or burlap over the fresh concrete and covering that with plastic. If the area is too big, use a hose to sprinkle it three times a day.

ESCAPE VALVE

Your bright idea: It's autumn and time to shut off the valve to your outdoor tap before the temperature drops—only you discover it has already frozen. You cut out the valve, splice in new pipe, and solder the unit in place.

The dismal result: The heat from your torch can damage internal components if the valve is shut. Now, the valve lets water pass through no matter how much you torque down the stem.

Next time around: Make sure it's open—or remove the guts—before sweating the joints. Also, direct the torch toward the pipe and away from the valve.

(cont.) TIPS OF THE TRADE:
QUICK FIXES FOR EASY MISTAKES

MAKING THE CUT
Your bright idea: It's pruning time, so you trim back trees by making clean cuts flush with the trunk.

The dismal result: You've removed the ridge at the base of the limb known as the branch collar; its protective cells are uniquely adapted to closing wounds. Disease soon causes your trees to wither.

Next time around: Look for the swollen ring at the base of the branch and cut as close to that as possible. To minimize damage on live growth, use bypass pruners.

TAKING SIDINGS
Your bright idea: Grime has accumulated on your once-pristine vinyl siding, so you paint a nice dark red over it.

The dismal result: Dark colors absorb more heat, a phenomenon called thermal pickup. A year later, the siding buckles and the paint begins to blister and flake off.

Next time around: Stick close to the siding's original color when repainting. If your siding is dark colored to begin with, there's no harm in following suit.

QUICK FIX

CHOOSE ECO-FRIENDLY SIDING
When the time comes to upgrade from the vinyl siding, consider materials that are both renewable and that will stand the test of time. Cement-based siding such as stucco and fiber cement provide durability and affordability. Aluminum and steel compositions are sophisticated and modern, and are often made from recyclable materials. While wood is a popular choice, it requires frequent maintenance, and should always be purchased from an FSC-certified source. Remember to research the entire ecological footprint when purchasing new siding. Something manufactured nearby will be cheaper to ship—and avoids unnecessary CO_2 emissions. If you're not yet ready to replace the vinyl, consider painting with a low– or no-VOC paint.

ADD A GREEN ROOF

FUTURE INVESTMENT

Now available for sloped roofs, a green roof contains several lightweight layers, including a waterproof membrane, a drainage layer, soil, and organic plant life. A green roof lowers your energy bills, reduces stormwater runoff, and is low-maintenance. Hire an architect or engineer to confirm your home's structural integrity will not be compromised with the addition of a low-maintenance green roof. Proper insulationing and lining the organic roof properly is necessary to keep unwelcome insects and other creatures from visiting you inside your home. Two resources for green roofs are Green Grid (greengrid.com) and Greenroofs for Healthy Cities(greenroofs.com). The cost of a green roof can range from $14 to $40 sq. ft and higher.

PREVENT ROOF MOLD AND MILDEW

In the spring or fall, install zinc strips on the roof ridge to prevent and eliminate unwanted mold and moss. Left untreated, the growth can lift the shingles and break down the underlayment. Mold grows in dark damp conditions, so cutting back overhanging shade trees can also help alleviate recurring mold problems.

* Illustration shows inproper use of a pressure washer.

1. Apply your soap- based agent to the roof using a garden sprayer, mop, or brush. Proceed cautiously when applying chemicals for any purpose, and try the least toxic product you can find first. Avoid chlorine bleach: it can remove the natural color from wood roofing, accelerate corrosion of metal gutter and downspout systems, and kill vegetation once it runs onto the ground. No matter what you use, try it on the least visible part of the roof first.

2. After the moss is dead, it can be carefully flushed off the roof with a pressure washer. The pressure washer has to be pointed down the roof or else you run the risk of driving water under the shingles. You'll have to actually

Cost: $38.50 for 50 ft.
Monthly Savings: Variable
Payback: Increased home value

stand on the roof to do this, which makes this a potentially dangerous job.

3. After the roof is clear, install zinc strips at the peak and at down-roof intervals to inhibit future moss growth. The strips release zinc carbonate into rainwater washing over the roof. The chemical is deposited on the shingle granules and prevents or greatly reduces moss growth.

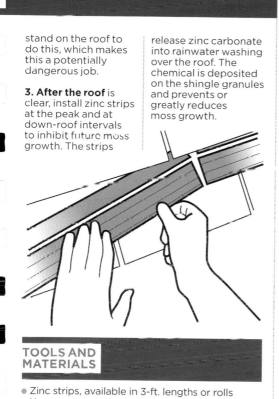

TOOLS AND MATERIALS

- Zinc strips, available in 3-ft. lengths or rolls
- Hammer
- Roofing nails
- Ladder
- Push broom or garden sprayer
- Pressure washer
- Nontoxic soap-based agent

TIPS OF THE TRADE:
STAINED VINYL SIDING

While vinyl is far from eco-friendly, before you strip off your stained siding off, replace it, and consign your old siding to a landfill, consider some elbow grease to remove the stains. There are very few things that can permanently stain vinyl.

The Vinyl Siding Institute suggests cleaning siding with a soft cloth or ordinary long-handled, soft bristle brush. For textured surfaces, use only a soft-bristle brush to keep the grooves in the texture stain free. Start at the bottom of the house and work up and rinse your cleaning solution completely before it dries. If your house has a combination of brick facing and vinyl siding, make sure to cover the brick so that it is not affected by the runoff.

You can use a power washer to clean but should carefully read instructions before use. At no point should you aim the power washer upward, as water may be driven behind the siding, causing buckling and forcing moisture to accumulate. Follow the siding manufacturer's recommendations as well, as they vary greatly. Some manufacturers don't want pressure washers used on their products at all. Others allow them, but have limitations on the amount of pressure and the cleaners that can be used. Most will caution against the use of pressure washers around any opening in the wall, such as windows, doors, electrical wiring, and plumbing.

An effective cleaner of mold and mildew is a mixture of 30percent vinegar and 70percent water. For other stains, the Vinyl Siding Institute provides this list of suggested household cleaners. Because few of these cleaners are eco-friendly, try using the vinegar and water mixture first before resorting to harsh chemicals.

THE EXTERIOR OF YOUR HOME

STAIN	CLEANERS
BUBBLE GUM	FANTASTIK, MURPHY OIL SOAP, SOLUTION OF VINEGAR (30%), WATER (70%) AND WINDEX
CRAYON	LESTOIL
DAP (OIL-BASED CAULK)	FANTASTIK
FELT-TIP PEN	FANTASTIK, WATER-BASED CLEANERS
GRASS	FANTASTIK, LYSOL, MURPHY OIL SOAP, WINDEX
LITHIUM (CAR) GREASE	FANTASTIK, LESTOIL, MURPHY OIL SOAP, WINDEX
MOTOR OIL	FANTASTIK, LYSOL, MURPHY OIL SOAP, WINDEX
PAINT	BRILLO PAD, SOFT SCRUB
PENCIL	SOFT SCRUB
RUST	FANTASTIK, MURPHY OIL SOAP, WINDEX
TAR	SOFT SCRUB

Patios and Driveways

The area surrounding your home may already have a combination of hard-scapes (patios, decks, walkways and driveways) and plant life. A landscape architect can help maximize the outdoor living space around your home with permeable materials (such as pervious pavement, gravel, or paving stones), and landscaping designed to absorb rain water runoff (such as rain barrels and man-made swales). There are 25 million acres of impervious ground surfaces in the U.S. where rainfall runs off rather than soaking into the ground. This runoff carries fertilizers, pesticides, eroded soil, and organic material into storm sewers and from there into waterways, damaging natural eco-systems and contaminating drinking water.

KNOW YOUR STUFF:
DRY WELLS

A dry well built to accept water from a downspout is often just a large hole in the ground covered with boards and filled with rocks to keep the sides from collapsing. A better dry well, however, is a clean steel or plastic drum buried 18 in. below grade, at least 10 ft. from the house's foundation. Do not bury the drum closer, because runoff seeping from it could enter the house's basement through cracks in the foundation.

Drill numerous holes through the drum with a 1/2-in.-diameter drill bit, and fill the drum with medium-size stones. Make the drum's lid from pressure-treated lumber or a thin slab of concrete reinforced with wire. This design is better than a rock-filled hole because it is less likely to fill with silt eroded from the soil.

A dry well should work in most situations because its large surface area allows water to percolate into the ground before the drum is filled with water. However, if your area has high ground-water levels in some seasons, or year round, there will be times when the drum is filled with water and can't accept runoff. Also, a dry well can become ineffective if it fills with debris washed out of a house's gutters, so it's important to keep your gutters clean.

The amount of water any dry well can accept depends on the size of the well and the percolation rate of the soil. A hydrologist can determine the amount of water entering the dry well by taking into account the rate of the rainfall, the roof area, the size of the gutter channel, and the cross-sectional area of the downspout. However, most homeowners are realists and not theoreticians. If one dry well is not effective, they put in a second and a third.

Dry wells can be installed in series or in parallel. When installed in series, each well has an outlet near its top. If the dry well fills up before the water can leach into the ground, the water flows through the outlet to the next well. When dry wells are installed in parallel, a distribution box—similar to that used in a septic system—is installed. The box, which is plastic or masonry, has an inlet from the downspout and two or three outlets, each going to a dry well. The dry wells should be spaced so that they have enough soil around them to absorb all the water they will receive.

GREEN YOUR DRIVEWAY OR PATIO

Blacktop and concrete crack as the ground beneath expands and contracts and requires repaving regularly. Putting in an eco-friendly alternative such as permeable pavers will create a surface that lasts significantly longer with little maintenance and allows your yard to better absorb rainfall. House bricks are not suitable if the paved area is a parking space or driveway; concrete bricks, typically slightly smaller, will be durable under these severe conditions.

1: Unless the brick path is laid against a wall or similar structure, the edges of the paving must be contained by a permanent restraint, such as lumber treated with chemical preservative. The edging boards should be flush with the surface of the path, but drive the stakes so that they can be covered by soil or turf. Concrete paving will need a more substantial edging of bricks set in concrete. Provide a slope for water runoff on patios and drives.

2: Lay brick walkways and patios on a 3-in.-thick gravel base, covered with a 2-in. layer of compacted, slightly damp sharp sand. When the bricks are first laid on the sand, they should project ⅜-in. above the edging restraints. When laying concrete bricks for a drive, you need to increase the depth of the gravel to 6 in. Fully compact the gravel so that sand from the bedding course is not lost in the subbase.

3: When the area of paving is complete, run the vibrating plate over the surface two or three times until it has worked the bricks down into the sand flush with the outer edging. Complete the job by brushing more kiln-dried, joint-filling sand across the finished paving and vibrating it into the open joints.

THE EXTERIOR OF YOUR HOME

TOOLS AND MATERIALS

- Brick pavers
- Sand
- Gravel
- Shovel
- Pick
- Gloves
- Two-by-Fours the size of the perimeter of your project
- Stakes
- Plate compactor

Cost: $2 to $5 per sq. ft.
Monthly Savings: $0
Payback: Increased home value

FUTURE INVESTMENT

XERISCAPE LANDSCAPING

Conserves natural resources by replacing water hogs such as turf grass with native plants appropriate to your local climate. By using water-conserving landscaping solutions such as integrating the hardscapes and the organic parts of your yard, creating swales, and building terraced patios or decks with plant life, xeriscaping minimizes water run-off and evaporation and works to eliminate the need for supplemental irrigation. Professional Landscape Architects are available to help guide you through this process. While this type of landscaping is pricy and requires more start-up work than a traditional lawn, the many advantages include lower water bills, little to no lawnmowing, and optimization of outdoor living space.

Lawn and Garden

The great American lawn is entirely man-made—yet it covers over 50 million acres in North America alone. The verdant, closely cropped, always lush dream lawn requires an extraordinary amount of fertilizer, water, and human energy to look just right, not to mention the gasoline needed to mow it. Many alternatives to the traditional lawn are available in today's market, and most are considerably less costly and less time consuming. But if you want to keep that lawn green and well-manicured, there are steps you can take to save money and be a little more eco-friendly in the process. Here are some easy changes you can implement immediately.

MOWER MAKEOVER

1: Go Electric. There are currently several powerful electric mowers that provide up to an hour of maneuverable mowing. Be advised: while you're cutting down on gas costs, this will increase your electric bill.

Cost: $50 to $450
Monthly Savings: $10
Payback: 5 to 45 months

2: Use a Mulching Mower. Yard waste makes up 13 percent of residential garbage, and over one-third of it goes into landfills. Use a mulching mower to return finely chopped grass—and valuable nitrogen and moisture—to your lawn instead. In the fall, a mower can either mulch leaves directly into the yard or bag the particles. They break down quickly in a compost pile.

3: Think Manual. There's no need to use a gas mower if your lawn is tiny. Manual mowers are lighter than ever, with smooth-cutting, efficient blades. They can give you a brisk workout to the fragrance of fresh-cut grass—minus the gas.

SAY NO TO MOWING

How does an entire summer of no mowing sound? Pretty good. All you have to do is step back and let the meadow grow. Meadows are best created in sunny areas of the lawn and will require little maintenance if native grasses or flowers are selected.

1: Simply stop mowing an existing part of your lawn. You can help to jump start the meadow by planting native plants and flowers. The grass will grow tall and produce seeds, and wildflowers will begin to grow. It will take several years before the meadow takes on a pleasant appearance, so you'll need to have some patient neighbors.

2: If you want to try this in just part of your yard. Choose the sunniest spot. Even a small meadow will attract an abundance of insects, birds, and other important members of your local eco-system.

PERFORM A SOIL TEST

Check the acidity or alkalinity of your lawn's soil by performing a soil test. (Do-it-yourself soil kits are sold at garden shops and hardware stores for about $15.) A value of 6.5 is ideal. If the soil is slightly acidic, raise the pH level by using a drop spreader to add pulverized lime to the lawn. To lower the pH of moderately alkaline soils, add organic material such as peat moss. For soil with extremely high pH, amend it with sulfur or iron sulfate.

QUICK FIX

REGULAR RAKING

Raking is a necessity for a healthy lawn. It's important to remove leaves in the fall and seed pods, pine cones, twigs, and spent flowers all year long. Debris, whether a thick layer of leaves or a thin layer of seed pods, blocks sunlight and reduces water absorption. This material can also dull the blade of a mower that works through it.

PLANT A TREE

According to the U.S. Department of Agriculture, 1 acre of trees produces 4 tons of oxygen annually. That's enough oxygen to sustain eighteen people for one full year. Trees act as carbon sinks by absorbing or sequestering carbon dioxide from the air, and leafy tree canopies intercept fine-particulate pollution and absorb pollutant such as nitrogen dioxide, ammonia, carbon monoxide, and sulfur dioxide. What you probably don't know is that trees can also save you money. Strategically planted trees can block out solar heat gain and keep your home cooler. Plant trees on the west and east sides of your house to reduce air-conditioning costs. In winter, evergreens can create wind-breaks, which can cut heating bills by as much as 30 percent.

HERE COMES THE RAIN

Another way to prevent runoff—and to avoid using the sump pimp—is to divert water from your gutters to a rain garden—a 6-in.-deep depression filled with water-loving plants. A properly designed garden will absorb standing water within hours, so it won't turn into a mosquito breeding ground.

1: Site It. Plant the garden on a gentle slope (less than 12 degrees) at least 10 ft. from the house. To test the soil, dig a 6-in. hole and fill it with water. If there's still standing water after 24 hours, the soil isn't permeable enough.

2: Dig It. The garden should be about 15 percent as big as the area it drains for sandy soil, more for silt or clay soil. When digging, tie a string between two stakes and use a carpenter's level to make sure the bottom of the garden is flat. Use the soil you excavate to build a gentle berm on the three downslope sides of the garden.

3: Plant It. The right mix of plants depends on where you live. Sedges and ferns are popular choices; gardeners can add a mix of perennials and shrubs. Some trees, including red maple and river birch, are suitable. Add 2 in. of mulch after planting.

Cost: $50 to $200
Monthly Savings: $6.25
Payback: 8 to 32 months

THE EXTERIOR OF YOUR HOME

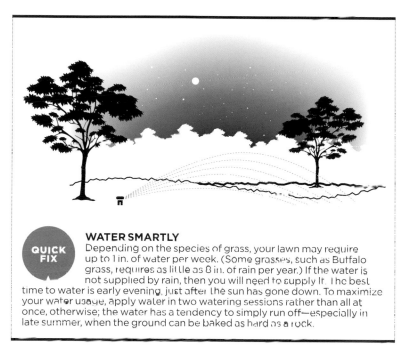

QUICK FIX

WATER SMARTLY

Depending on the species of grass, your lawn may require up to 1 in. of water per week. (Some grasses, such as Buffalo grass, requires as little as 8 in. of rain per year.) If the water is not supplied by rain, then you will need to supply it. The best time to water is early evening, just after the sun has gone down. To maximize your water usage, apply water in two watering sessions rather than all at once, otherwise; the water has a tendency to simply run off—especially in late summer, when the ground can be baked as hard as a rock.

TRY AN ORGANIC FERTILIZER

Use organic lawn-care products such as corn gluten meal that will suppress weeds as they fertilize. Because natural products lack the chemical potency of synthetic blends, they are also less likely to do damage if they are incorrectly applied. They are more expensive than synthetic products, but you will have a healthier lawn in the long run. Bear in mind that both natural and synthetic products are concentrated chemicals in terms of their environmental impact, so even organic fertilizer can contribute to water pollution. Don't over-apply and always carefully sweep up fertilizer that falls on a paved surface.

▶ WEEKEND PROJECT

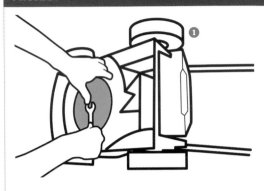

SHARPEN THE BLADES

You use less water, fertilizer, and fuel if you keep your mower's blades sharpened. Dull blades also rip the grass rather than cutting it, and leave behind jagged ends that quickly turn brown. Sharpen your blades every spring, and they should cut cleanly throughout the summer. Start with a mower that has an empty or nearly empty gas tank and make sure the gas cap is firmly tightened.

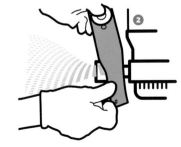

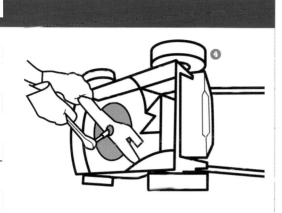

QUICK FIX

USE LESS FERTILIZER

Reduce the amount of fertilizer you use and you will probably need to water less often. Fertilizer and other lawn chemicals can actually make your lawn thirstier.

1: Disconnect the spark plug wire and tip the mower on its side. Use a wrench and remove the blade.

2: Wearing work gloves, use a mill file (about $9 at any hardware store) to smooth out damage and sharpen the edge. Maintain the bevel at 40 to 45 degrees.

3: Test the blade for balance by placing it on a cone-shaped blade balancer (about $5 at hardware stores), or drive a nail into your workbench and hang the blade from the hole in its center. On the balancer or the nail, the blade should hang evenly. If it tips to one side, remove metal from the opposite side.

4: Replace the blade, refuel the mower, and test on a firm, level surface to check for vibration before cutting grass.

Cost: $15
Monthly Savings: $10
Payback: 2 months

DON'T LET BROWN PATCHES BUG YOU

Regardless of whether you use municipal or well water, be sensible about your irrigation and conserve water. Irrigate only the portions of the lawn that are highly stressed or that most contribute to the house's landscape. Don't sweat it when a lawn turns brown and brittle during a dry spell or even an outright drought. Healthy lawns go dormant from a lack of water. They bounce back when rainfall returns.

HUG A TREE

Gardening and groundwork do not come to a standstill in the winter. There is work to do, such as tree care. Trees experience a period of dormancy during the winter months, so this is an ideal time to do minor pruning and other small jobs. There are three things you can do during the winter months to ensure healthier trees, according to the International Society of Arboriculture (ISA), a nonprofit group that oversees the tree care industry and acts as an advocate for proper tree care. (isa-arbor.com)

1: Protect new plants by covering up with mulch. Spread a thin layer of mulch around the base of trees, especially young ones or those that are newly planted. Ideally, this should be done during the fall. If you haven't mulched yet, you might give it a try, especially if your area encounters a midwinter thaw or is experiencing a mild winter.

2: Remove deadwood and lightly prune. Remove dead or damaged branches and perform limited greenwood pruning of declining and poorly placed branches. This should be done with as minimal an amount of cutting as possible.

3: Water strategically. If your area normally experiences a mild winter or if you are experiencing a mild, dry winter where you live, the trees could benefit from water. Water where soils and trees are cool but not frozen, and where there has been little precipitation.

Cost: $4 per cu. ft.
Monthly Savings: $0
Payback: Save on tree replacement

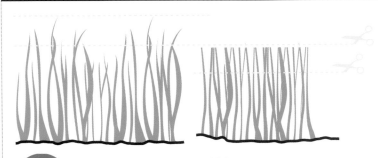

TAKE A LITTLE OFF THE TOP

QUICK FIX

Adjust the height of the mower's deck to the top or second-highest position. Time your mowing so that you remove about one-third of the grass blades each time you mow. In the early spring that may mean mowing every four or five days. In the summer, once a week should do it. In late summer, you may not need to mow at all if the grass goes dormant and stops growing. Trimming grass too short lops off much of the energy-producing top growth, resulting in a weak, sickly lawn that will require more of your time, water, and maintenance. Frequent mowing to the correct height will also produce tiny grass clippings that may be left on the lawn to decompose and return nutrients back to the soil.

ARE YOU MULCHING CORRECTLY?

QUICK FIX

To plant a new shrub or tree, dig a hole two or three times the root diameter, backfill halfway, water, then fill the remaining depth. Mulch suppresses weeds and con-serves moisture, but you can overdo it. A couple of inches on top are enough. Don't cover the root flare—the point where the stem meets the roots.This denies the plant air and traps moisture where it doesn't belong.

► **WEEKEND PROJECT**

RECYCLE WATER
Wastewater from nontoilet plumbing is referred to as gray water. Many commercial buildings use gray water from sinks to perform functions such as flushing toilets. Different communities are experimenting with expanding their use of gray water into other areas of the home and garden.

1: Gravity Drum
The DIY-friendly gravity drum directs water from a washing machine into mulch basins (not sprinklers) to irrigate trees and shrubs. Home-owners should check plumbing codes, and avoid using detergents with boron, sodium, or chlorine. Visit Oasis Design for guidance on creating your own. (oasisdesign.net)

2: Restrictions
Don't use gray water from the kitchen because it likely contains contaminates

from bacteria and chemicals. Don't reuse shower or bath water, and never use water that has come in contact with the toilet, or from a bidet or urinal. There are other health precautions you should follow if you have a vegetable garden.

Cost: $195
Monthly Savings: Variable
Payback: Lowered water bill

QUICK FIX

LADIES WHO MUNCH
Ladybugs aren't just pretty—they're useful, too, snacking on aphids and other garden pests. Purchase ladybugs from your garden supply store and set them loose. Repeat the release of ladybugs two or three times a season. To attract local ladybugs, try planting their favorites: fennel and cilantro.

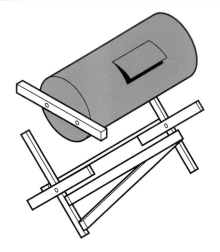

BUILD A ROTATING COMPOSTING BIN

According to the EPA, Americans throw out 25 percent of their food—96 billion pounds of leftovers—every year. When these organic materials decompose in anaerobic (without oxygen) conditions in our landfills, they produce methane, a greenhouse gas 21 times more potent than carbon dioxide. Help divert organic materials from the landfill and make your own compost at the same time by building a rotating bin. The rotation will not only speed the composting process, it will keep it rodentfree. Once assembled, fill it two-thirds full with scraps, moisten with water, and rotate every few days.

1. Mark an opening on the side of a food-grade barrel using masking tape. Bore a $3/8$-in.-diameter hole at each of its corners and use a jigsaw with a metal-cutting blade to cut out the shape of the door. Clean up the edges of the door and barrel with a file.

2: Attach the door to the barrel. Use screws or bolts to fasten metal hinges or make a flap hinge from scraps of bicycle inner tube. Screw a couple of small blocks to the inside of the barrel to keep the door from falling in, and another on the outside to act as a latch.

3: Make two X-shaped stands using scrap lumber 2 x 4s. Fasten the Xs together with bolts, screws, or nails that are bent over where they exit. Connect the two X-shaped stands with horizontal lumber, and add diagonal braces to keep them steady.

4: Attach a wooden turning lever to the end of the barrel using large sheet metal screws or bolts. Rub wax or a piece of candle on the components of the wooden stand that make contact with the barrel to lubricate them.

TOOLS AND MATERIALS

- Food-grade barrel
- Masking tape
- Jigsaw with a metal cutting blade
- File
- Several small blocks
- Two scrap 2 x 4s
- Bolts, nails, screws
- Hinges or old bicycle inner tube
- Diagonal braces
- Large sheet metal screws
- Bar of soap (for lubricating)

Cost: $100
Monthly Savings: $10
Payback: 10 months

QUICK FIX

USE A RAIN BARREL
Containers to collect rainwater date back 2,000 years—and are just as useful today. Directing your downspout to a rain barrel will not only reduce runoff but also provide water for your lawn and garden.

MONEY-SAVING HOME IMPROVEMENTS

 Remodeling projects can take a financial and an emotional toll on you and your family. Whether it's in the kitchen, the basement, or your bedroom, daily life is disrupted as the work goes on. But when it's finished, your quality of life improves. When the time comes for a remodeling project, keep it green.

KNOW YOUR STUFF
LURKING BELOW THE SURFACE

LOOK BEFORE YOU LEAP. THERE ARE LOTS OF THINGS IN A WALL THAT CAN STOP A JOB DEAD IN ITS TRACKS. HERE'S A BRIEF PRIMER ABOUT WHAT YOU MIGHT SEE WHILE REMODELING.

Sheetmetal Duct. If there's one thing that can foul up your plans, it's duct. Rerouting a short, simple length can be a DIY endeavor, but dealing with long lengths or complex transitions usually calls for a pro.

Cast-Iron, PVC Pipe. Large plastic or cast-iron drain wastewater or allow sewer gas to escape through roof vents. Rerouting these is a big job. If you find cast-iron, plan on transitioning to PVC. It's easier to work with.

Insulation. Insulation is found only in exterior walls (unless it's being used for soundproofing). Removing it will create cold spots and also cause condensation to form, leading to moisture damage.

Protector Plates. Steel protector plates (1/16 in. thick) are hammered to the face of a stud to protect wiring or plumbing that's run through the framing. If you hit metal when drilling into a wall, stop and find another place to drill.

Fasteners. It's not unusual to hit lots of nails or screws when removing drywall. Panels are attached with Type W coarse-thread screws, at least 1-1/4 in. long, or ring-shank nails, at least 1-1/4 in. long.

Building
Materials

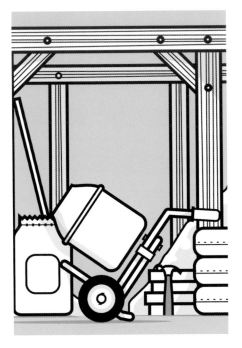

When the time comes to select materials for a remodeling project, be greenminded. A multitude of eco-materials are now available that are as good for the environment as they are for your bank account (for example, wood certified from sustainably managed forests, or products made from recycled materials). Consider reusing or salvaging items rather than paying for virgin materials.

PURCHASE DECONSTRUCTION MATERIALS

The salvage business is a big business, allowing you to buy used materials for virtually any home-related project. Keep in mind that some materials (such as windows and toilets) should be purchased new, as old ones may not be code compliant.

1: Inspect the materials you are interested in closely before you purchase. Keep an eye out for lead paint, embedded fasteners, or other flaws.

2: Avoid paying extra for long-distance shipping by seeking out local sources. Several companies such as Renew Salvage (renewsalvage.org) will provide you with current information and items available online.

MAKE YOUR OWN
WALLPAPER PASTE

If you are planning to wallpaper, be aware that most wallpaper paste emits the fumes of volatile compounds, which can cause irritated eyes, difficulty breathing, and nausea. Make your own paste and avoid the headache. This recipe can be stored in a glass or ceramic container for up to four weeks in the fridge.

2: Pour water slowly into the flour mixture, constantly stirring the mixture into a heavy cream. Turn the burner to a medium heat and stir as the mixture turns into a thick paste.

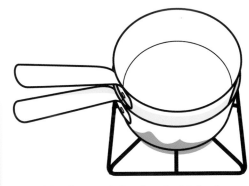

1: Combine flour and alum in a double broiler on the stove (in the inside pan.) Add water to 3 in. below the top of the outside pan.

Cost: $10
Monthly Savings: $10
Payback: Immediate

TOOLS AND MATERIALS

- Double boiler
- Quart-size glass or ceramic-lidded container
- Water
- 3 cups wheat flour
- 6 teaspoons alum
- 2 tablespoons clove oil

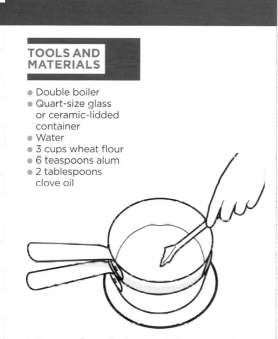

3: Remove from the heat and allow to cool completely. Stir in the clove oil. This makes 3 cups of paste.

SUPPORT A NONPROFIT

When you buy your salvaged materials from nonprofit organizations such as Habitat for Humanity, you practice recycling—and save yourself money—while supporting an organization performing good works in the community. Habitat for Humanity sells a wide variety of used building supplies, and all profits go to support their building programs. (habitatforhumanity.org)

KNOW YOUR STUFF:
HOW TO HIRE A CONTRACTOR
(AND AVOID SCAMMERS)

We love building for ourselves, but some jobs just need to be subbed out. Unfortunately, a competent, honest remodeling contractor is no easy find. There are thousands of reliable, trustworthy contractors out there—but there are quite a few toolbox-wielding knuckleheads, too. To protect yourself—and your money—here are some tips to ensure that your next remodeling project goes smoothly.

AVOID SHADY TACTICS
The first thing to do is make sure you're not being scammed. Beware these ten red flags. The contractor:

- Provides credentials or references that can't be verified.

- Offers a special price, but only if you sign a contract today.

- Accepts only cash, requires large deposits, or wants the entire cost up front.

- Asks you to write a check in his name (not to the business).

- Won't provide a written contract or complete bid.

- Refuses to apply for building permits, and asks you to get them.

- Offers exceptionally long warranties.

- Proposes to do most or all of the work on weekends and afterhours.

- Gives you a low-ball offer that sounds too good to be true.

- Has "Will work for beer" painted on the side of his trucks.

CHECK THE CONSTRUCTION WORK
When you meet with contractors, ask each to bring photos or drawings of completed jobs that are similar to yours. When possible, ask to visit a completed project. Get in touch with the homeowners involved.

Vetting a contractor through customers works both ways—word-of-mouth recommendations have long been one of the most reliable means of finding competent contractors. Seek references from neighbors, friends, architects, colleagues, and real estate agents.

CHECK THE PAPERWORK

Check to make sure contractors are licensed and insured. A good pro should volunteer documentation. If you have doubts, contact the Better Business Bureau and check for complaints. When comparing competitors' bids, make sure everything is spelled out. This includes the scope of the work, materials specified, warranties, references, time frames, cost overruns, payment schedule and price.

Once you have chosen a contractor, obtain a written contract that includes the items specified in the original bid, plus the final price, payment terms, sales tax, permit fees, the specific work to be performed, materials to be used, warranties, start and end date, change order processes, final review and sign-off procedures, and debris removal. Once the job is under way, make sure the necessary building permits are on display.

CHECK THE BILLS

When advancing money for materials, ask the contractor if you can pay the supplier directly. Always pay with a check, never by cash. Take a carrot-and-stick approach to completed work—pay incrementally as each significant phase of work is completed. Be careful about paying for work that hasn't been finished. Before making the final payment, do a visual inspection of the entire project and make a punch list of any repairs or uncompleted work. Put all change orders in writing; avoid verbal contracts.

A small but important technicality: request signed lien releases from all major subcontractors and suppliers before making final payments. A lien release guarantees that the contractor has fully paid his materials suppliers. Even if you've paid the contractor, he might not have paid the supplier. Get those lien releases.

ECO-FRIENDLY SURFACE MATERIALS

Choose the materials for your home projects carefully. Selecting long-lasting, eco-friendly materials can increase both your home's value and your quality of life.

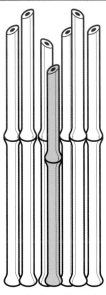

1: Stone

Although stone seems like a good alternative, it's not all that durable or sanitary. Stone is porous, making it vulnerable to water, food particles, and bacteria. As a result, some manufacturers will coat the stone with a high-VOC sealant. The adhesive products used in stone installation are usually epoxy based and therefore also extremely high in VOCs. If you must have the granite countertop, be sure to select a nontoxic alternative. ($60 to $120 per sq. ft.)

2: Glass

Recycled glass mixed with a cement, concrete, or resin base creates an incredibly durable surface material for floors and countertops. Some products are mixed with fly ash, which is a waste product of burning coal, making this an even better eco-choice. ($85 to $150 per sq. ft.)

3: Paper

one hundred-percent post-consumer recycled waste paper combined with water-based, petroleum-free resin is another eco-option for your countertops or floors. If you are handling the installation yourself, you will be delighted by how easy this type of countertop is to work with. ($25 to $55 per sq. ft.)

4: Bamboo

Bamboo is a popular substitute for wood because it's a fast-growing renewable resource and very durable. Look into the origin of the product before making a purchase, and be wary of how far the product will be shipped to get to you. You want to purchase from a local supplier and be sure it is harvested in a responsible manner. ($30 per sq. ft. or more)

5: Cork
Cork, which is the outer bark stripped from cork trees, is a renewable resource, inexpensive, and easy to install. Cork makes great floors, countertops, and even walls. Cork will never be as durable or last as long as wood or stone, but it is perfect for a quick upgrade. ($25 per sq. ft. or more)

7: Linoleum
Sometimes confused with vinyl flooring, linoleum is a surprisingly eco-friendly option made from flax seed oil. It comes in a wide range of colors and patterns, and is inexpensive and very easy to install. ($6 per sq. ft. or more)

8: Virgin Wood
Affordable options for responsibly forested wood are widely available. If you are purchasing virgin wood, look for Forest Stewardship Council-certified wood, which will be 100 percent formaldehyde-free and harvested only

from forests or plantations that are sustainably managed. ($60 per sq. ft. or more)

9: Salvaged Wood
Salvaged or reclaimed wood is another cost-effective option. Avoid laminated products (these often contain formaldehyde). When inspecting the planks, be on the lookout for lead paint, and be aware that until 2004, arsenic was widely used as a preservative in pressure-treated lumber ($40 per sq. ft. or more)

10: Stainless Steel
Eco-friendly steel has long been the choice for professional kitchens because of its affordability, durability, and resistance to bacteria. Look for a stainless steel high in recycled content and remember—if you choose to replace it down the line, it is fully recyclable. ($50 to $75 per sq. ft.)

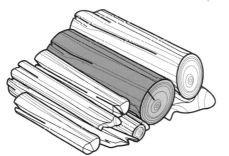

CHANGE YOUR CEILING LIGHTS

Light-emitting diode lighting fixtures can provide up to 60 lumens per watt—50 percent more than the best compact fluorescent. You can easily replace all of your recessed lights with LEDS. Although it will cost you more money up front, the burn time is 50,000 hours—five times as long as traditional bulbs. Also, the heat emitted into the room is significantly lower. You'll feel the difference, and see the savings on your next electricity bill.

FUTURE INVESTMENT

CHANGE YOUR WALLS

There are now a variety of affordable materials that are both healthy for the indoor environment and easy to work with that homeowners can use to upgrade their wall coverings.

1: Low-VOC Paint

The solvents and amines used in latex paints are known as volatile organic compounds (VOCs). VOCs are considered harmful if inhaled in high concentrations, which is why it's important to ventilate a room when painting. More than 50 percent of the VOCs in paint are still being emitted one year after painting, and can cause headaches, sore throats, nausea, and drowsiness. Most manufacturers offer low-VOC paints. You won't spend more on low- or no-VOC paint, and the quality will be similar.

2: Milk or Soy Paint

Two other alternatives to latex are milk- and soy-based paints. Milk paint is a very old style of paint that derives its stability from milk protein. It is a fast-drying and water-soluble paint. (milkpaint. com). Soy paint is also nontoxic and can be safely used both indoors and outdoors. (ecosafetyproducts. com)

3: Clay

Clay contains none of the toxic compounds found in paints and traditional plasters and comes in a variety of colors and textures. The application (simply mix it up, trowel it on, and rework to your liking) is headache free. (americanclay.com)

4: Wallpaper

When selecting wallpaper, make sure you purchase a wood-based lining paper rather than one produced using PVC. Alternatives include PVC-free silk-screened paper, wallpaper made from recycled paper, and textile wall coverings like those made from bark and sisal.

Remodeling

Whether you're trying to sell your home, add to its value, or update for a new look, it can all be done with conservation and the environment in mind. The projects in this section help promote the reuse and recycle mantra in ways you may not previously have considered.

QUICK FIX

CHECK FOR ASBESTOS AND LEAD

Before you get started with any construction, ensure your home is free of asbestos and lead paint. Both were frequently used in the construction of homes built between 1900 and 1970. There is no completely safe method for "do-it-yourself" removal of lead-based paint, and each of the paint-removal methods—sandpaper, scrapers, chemicals, and torches or heat guns—can produce lead fumes or dust. While there are testing kits on the market, without a professional chemical analysis, it's impossible to tell if you have a problem, or how severe it is. If testing is unavailable or costly, assume older painted surfaces contain lead. Visit the EPA's Web site for details on asbestos and lead paint removal. (epa.gov)

QUICK FIX

ADD RADIANT FLOOR HEATING

Sometimes when you rip out old carpeting, you get lucky, and find pristine wooden floors underneath; but when the floor is above an unheated basement or crawlspace, it can be downright chilly during winter. Consider retrofitting with a staple-up radiant floor heating system, designed for wood framed floors. While it's considerably more expensive than forced-air heating systems, radiant floor heating is embedded under your floor and uses the entire floor to evenly distribute low-temperature heat for the most efficient form of heat available. It operates without a furnace, eliminating noise and dust, and requires significantly less operating time to maintain a comfortable temperature compared with a forced-air system, keeping your future operational costs to a minimum.

QUICK FIX

GET (NEW) OLD KITCHEN CABINETS

Replacing your kitchen cabinets may be the biggest remodeling investment you will make since the quality of your kitchen can make, or break a home sale. Before you lay down the considerable amount of money for new cabinets, take these things into consideration.

1: If you're buying new, skip the particleboard unless it has been coated with a primer/sealant paint; otherwise, the formaldehyde used in its manufacture will be released into the air and cause a potential health risk to you and your family. The quality is also subpar.

2: If you are considering custom cabinets (which can be a worthwhile investment since many home buyers look for custom), then using reclaimed wood is a great way to save money. But be sure you are buying quality lumber, and not just used particleboard. You can work directly with a cabinetmaker who will use reclaimed wood for you. Custom cabinets are never inexpensive, but you will likely recoup your investment when you sell your home. (elmwoodreclaimed timber.com)

3: Scout out vintage cabinets, especially when renovating an older house. Look online for companies that specialize in fine architectural items and vintage house parts (greatsalvage.com; oldegoodthings.com; historichouseparts. com)

4. Think about modular cabinets if you have a basic kitchen configuration. Modular cabinets are ideal when you use reclaimed timber because you can buy premade, high-quality cabinets for a fraction of the custom cabinet price. (greenteadesign. com)

Cost: $1,200 and up

Monthly Savings: $0

Payback: Increased home value

FUTURE INVESTMENT

PUT IN NEW WINDOWS
With single-glazed (single-pane) windows, you can lose up to twice as much heat as you with double-glazed windows. Triple glazing is about five times as efficient as single glazing. Custom triple-glazed windows can replace heat-leaking single-pane sash models and be almost as insulating as a wall. Energy Star-rated windows ensure lower utility bills, but think economically before you upgrade. Studies have shown that properly operating, weather-stripped single-glazed yields about the same savings as entry-level double-glazed windows of lesser quality.

● **Check local building codes** and requirements for placement and sizing. Retrofitting an old window with a newer model may result in a window that is too small. Following building code is essential; in the event of an emergency you will want your window large enough for a firefighter to enter, or for you to be able to escape.

● **Consider safety glass,** especially for entrance doors, French doors, or windows that are very close to the floor.

● **Window installation** is a tricky process, and the technique will vary depending on the type of window you are installing and the type of window you are removing. Hiring a manufacturer-approved contractor is always recommended.

KNOW YOUR STUFF
RENOVATING OLDER HOMES

Homeowners who have embarked on a major remodeling job—especially those involving the kitchen—quickly learn that older homes are electrically underpowered by modern standards. Many have only 60 or 100 amps of electrical service, while most newer homes have 200-amp service. Older homes generally did not have a trash disposal, dishwasher, hot-water dispenser, or multiple countertop outlets, all of which are common in modern kitchens.

To determine the extent of the electrical work necessary, you should hire a licensed electrical contractor. The contractor will examine the house's electrical system and perform load calculations. In some cases, the contractor may determine that the existing panel box can accommodate the new kitchen. But in other cases, a new subpanel box may be necessary. Large, complex remodeling jobs may require the installation of a new higher-amperage service cable and a larger higher-amperage panel box.

Specifically, if the inlet electrical service to your house is 100 amps, you cannot upgrade to 200 amps merely by changing the panel box to one rated for 200 amps. You must have the utility company bring a 200-amp cable to the weatherhead connection on the house. Next, your electrician must run a 200-amp cable from the weatherhead to the electrical meter, and from the meter to the new panel box. The branch circuits from the old box are relocated to the new box and additional branch circuits are added.

MONEY-SAVING HOME IMPROVEMENTS

All electrical work must meet local, state, and national electrical codes. When the job is done, the electrical contractor will provide you with a certificate of approval from the municipal inspection agency.

In addition to this new wiring, aluminum wiring poses a potential fire hazard. Between 1965 and 1973, about 1.5 million homes were wired with aluminum, which at the time was approved by the National Electrical Code. Later, it was found that dangerous overheating in 15- and 20-amp branch circuits at some connections between aluminum wires and outlets, switches, fixtures, and appliances resulted in fires. Anyone who has aluminum wiring should be alert for the following trouble signs:

- Cover plates on outlets or switches that are warm to the touch.

- Sparks, arching, or smoke at outlets or switches.

- Strange odors, especially the smell of burning plastic, around outlets and switches.

- Outlets, lights, or entire circuits that don't work.

Correcting the problem does not require rewiring the house, but repairs should be made by a licensed electrician who is familiar with the method recommended by the Consumer Product Safety Commission.

PAINT YOUR KITCHEN CABINETS

Don't rip those kitchen cabinets out just yet—a simple repainting job may do. Many older homes have sturdy carpenter-built cabinets that look outdated but may just need a fresh coat of paint.

1: Prepare by removing the drawers, adjustable shelves, and doors. Remove mounting screws from door hinges and drawer pulls and any additional hardware, such as door handles.

2: Use a sponge to thoroughly clean all cabinet surfaces using a cleaner called TSP substitute. Rinse the surfaces and let them dry, then fill dents and scratches with wood filler or drywall compound.

3: Lightly abrade surfaces to be painted with 120-grit sandpaper, then complete by applying painter's tape to surfaces you don't want painted, such as where the drawer box is mounted to the face.

TOOLS AND MATERIALS

- Paint
- Primer
- Paint tray
- Screwdriver
- Measuring tape
- Sponge
- Protective work gloves
- 120-grit sandpaper
- Sanding block
- Mini-paint roller
- Full-size paint roller
- Wood filler
- 2 to 2½ inch paintbrush
- 1-inch painter's tape
- New hardware (door handles and pulls)

4: Paint all of the surfaces with primer using a mini paint roller, which will paint into corners. Begin with the interior surfaces of the cabinets. Use a brush to coat the inside surface of the drawer faces and a full-size paint roller to coat doors, cabinet sides, and removable shelves. Use a brush to paint the cabinet face frames. Paint the inside edge of the frames, then paint the outer surface.

5: Once the primer is dry, repeat your painting steps with low-VOC paint. Let dry, them complete by reinstalling hardware, remounting the doors, and inserting the drawers.

Cost: $40

Monthly Savings: $0

Payback: Increased home value

TIPS OF THE TRADE:
SAVE YOUR FOUNDATION FROM WATER DAMAGE

If you have trouble with basement water, you're not alone. It's a big problem that often requires corrective action. What kind all depends on the source of the water.

WATER FROM ABOVE...

The most common cause of basement water is unmanaged rain runoff. Rainwater from the roof flows down through the soil and collects at the bottom of the original foundation excavation. While the weight of the saturated earth alone can break a wall, the situation worsens when the water freezes and exerts a lateral force that can cause cracks and buckling. How do you know when water damage is from runoff? When leaks follow substantial rains and when the soil around the foundation appears settled.

The solution is a well-maintained gutter system that uses downspout extensions to carry roof runoff at least 4 ft. from the foundation wall. Also, the grade next to the wall must be sloped to direct surface water away from the house.

...AND BELOW

Groundwater problems can result from a high water table or an underground spring. Sometimes the problem is seasonal, coinciding with spring snowmelts and heavier rains, but it can occur at any time. Groundwater doesn't usually break walls, but it can flood the basement floor.

Exterior drain tiles around the perimeter of the foundation footing are the first line of defense against groundwater. The simplest retrofit solution is to install a sump pump that carries the water away from the house. An interior drain-tile system is effective in routing water from the entire basement to the sump.

FOUNDATION REPAIR

If your foundation walls have cracks or they've buckled, you can do much of the repair work yourself or hire a contractor to handle the job. The newer techniques that use high-tech materials and sophisticated hardware require specialized skills, so you'll need to hire a professional.

Wall Rebuild. One solution to a buckled block wall is to replace it. You can do this without excavating. First, use post jacks and a 4 x 6 beam to take the load from the wall. Then, remove the damaged section down to the footing. After rebuilding the wall, wait several days before removing the jacks.

Excavation and Repair. To keep the original wall, excavate the area outside. Then, use a jack and a few wooden beams to nudge the wall back into position. Repair any bad mortar joints, and consider improving your drainage system to reduce hydrostatic pressure and to direct water away from the house.

Wall Bracing. If you don't want to replace the wall or excavate, try bracing. Vertical steel I-beams set in holes in the floor and fastened to steel braces at the ceiling joists can keep a wall in place. Local building codes vary, though, so make sure this approach is approved in your area.

Bracing with Belts. This system replaces I-beams with carbon-fiber/Kevlar belts (Fortress Stabilization Systems, 800-207-6204; fortressstabilization. com). A contractor grinds 1/8-in. recesses across the cracks. The belts are coated with epoxy and set in place, and the epoxy is trimmed flush with the wall.

Wall-Anchor Repair. Wall anchors (Grip-Tite Manufacturing, 515-462-1513; griptite.com) consist of two steel plates, one located on the inside of the wall and the other buried in the ground outside, and a threaded rod connecting the plates. Tightening a nut on the rod draws the wall flat.

Lifting Walls. When footings settle they can be repositioned with push piers (Foundation Pier System, Grip-Tite Manufacturing). Hydraulic drivers placed around 3 to 6 ft. apart push steel piers down to the bedrock while support brackets restore the footing to its original level.

REPLACE YOUR COUNTER-TOP

If your kitchen needs a facelift but your budget can't handle a major renovation, a new countertop may be the practical answer. Replacing an old, worn work surface can go a long way toward giving your kitchen a new lease on life. Swap in a reclaimed countertop or purchase new from our eco-friendly materials list on page 136-137. Here's the breakdown of your alternatives.

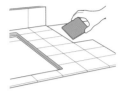

1: Relaminate your countertop. Just like a fresh coat of paint, a new layer of plastic laminate is a fast, low-budget way to quickly update and add value to your home. You can only relaminate a countertop with a flat backsplash or no backsplash, as bending laminate around small-radius corners can only be done at the factory.

2: Tile it. Ceramic tiles offer a richness of texture that no other countertop surface can match— in addition to being inexpensive, readily available, and easy to install. While it's more time consuming than other countertop installations, you can cover just about any surface with tile. Keep the grout clean by applying grout sealer according to the manufacturer's instructions.

QUICK FIX

GET LEED CERTIFIED
The LEED (Leadership in Energy and Environmental Design) certification program is a nationally accepted benchmark for green standards in both residential and commercial buildings. Visit the U.S. Green Building Council's Web site (usbc.org); you may find that you are entitled to certain tax incentives for home improvement projects. It also contains resources to help you obtain LEED certification (usbc.org)

3: Install a post-formed countertop.
Durable, stain-resistant, and inexpensive, they are now available with left- or right mitered ends and with sink openings partially cut. You'll also find matching endcaps, splice hardware, and build-up kits for counters where dishwashers are installed. If the additional expense is not an issue, consider ordering custom-cut lengths from a home center.

4: Install a solid-surface countertop
Different from laminate or tile countertops, where cutting produces a raw, exposed edge of plywood or particleboard, a solid-surface countertop is solid all the way through. It is the most expensive option available, especially if you choose a high-quality surface like granite or quartz, and you won't be able to install it yourself. Cutting, routing, and joining solid-surface materials is somewhat hazardous and best left to a professional.

TIPS OF THE TRADE:
INSTALL THE PERFECT SKYLIGHT

A skylight has lots of advantages, such as good looks and admiting plentiful daylight. While installing one is a complex project that involves reframing the ceiling, cutting rafters, drywall work, and sometimes working with complicated trim, the result can be breathtaking—and add value to your home.

FIRST PRIORITY: NO LEAKS
If you're not going the DIY route, hire a skylight specialist. Skylights are installed in one of two ways: either directly on the deck with mounting brackets or on a boxlike frame called a curb (best for roofs with a shallow pitch).

Curb-mounted units have step flashing around the frame to shed water. The flashing is made up of top and bottom caps and L-shaped side pieces that are woven into the shingle courses. Deck-mounted skylights are installed with step flashing, too. Flashing kits are available for various roof types such as tile, metal, and shakes. You'll also find easy-to-install self-flashing models that are suitable for asphalt-shingle roofs.

THE DIY SOLUTION
If you do the job yourself, choose a product with clear installation instructions, that you can check at a manufacturer's Web site or by calling its customer support number. An incorrect installation may cause leaks and void the skylight's warranty.

Here's an installer's trick that keeps a skylight high and dry: install a waterproof underlayment before the flashing and shingles go on.

"The adhesive-back underlayment runs from the plywood roof sheathing up the sides of the curb and effectively seals the hole cut in the roof," explains Todd Brown, vice president of Pacific Northwest Skylights, a Kirkland, Wash., firm that installs 500 skylights a year. Brown says watertight installation is ensured by wrapping the entire skylight assembly with the material.

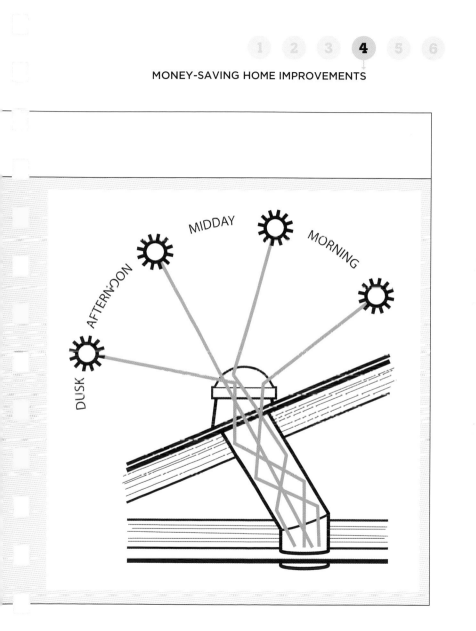

(cont.) TIPS OF THE TRADE:
INSTALL THE PERFECT SKYLIGHT

CHOOSING A SKYLIGHT

Preventing energy from leaking through the skylight is nearly as important as keeping water out. So it pays to choose an energy-efficient model. Most current skylights feature flat glass panels with argon gas sealed between them. A metal film (often referred to as low-E coating) applied to the glass further improves energy efficiency by reducing solar heat gain (and reduces bleaching of fabrics by the sun).

Another factor to look for is whether the skylight is fixed (nonopening) or venting (capable of opening, but more expensive). Try installing several skylights in a large room to save money on remodel.

However, some homeowners have discovered that it's possible to have too much of a good thing. A skylight that's too large means excessive heat gain in the summer and heavy heat loss in the winter. If the room has many windows, keep the skylight area to within 5 percent of the floor area. If there are few windows, you can go as high as 15 percent.

Adding features raises a skylight's cost significantly. Expect to pay $150 to $200 for a premium-quality 22 x 38-in., energy-efficient, fixed skylight. A manual-opening model costs $300. As an electrically opened skylight, that same model costs $600.

SHADE TOOLS

Even small skylights admit a tremendous amount of sunlight and heat—sometimes more than you want. For rooms requiring nearly total darkness, such as a bedroom, install blackout shades. These extra-thick roller shades block 95 to 98 percent of daylight and reduce cooling costs. Another open are aluminum miniblinds, which are fully adjustable and ideal for humid areas, such as bathrooms.

To reduce glare without darkening, consider cellular shades. These fabric shades have a light-diffusing honeycomb profile. For high-tech—and pricey—shade, Velux offers electronically tintable electrochromic glass. It adjusts the amount of light passing through with the click of a button.

QUICK FIX

THREE QUICK BATHROOM UPGRADES

If a new bathroom isn't in the near future for you, use these quick eco-fixes to improve the room's quality and appearance. Whiter sinks and tubs and shinier fixtures are just a trip to your hardware store and some elbow grease away.

1: Mineral deposits streak your sink, tub, and toilet. Regular cleaning will keep those streaks from becoming permanent stains. Use a nontoxic DIY cleaning solution such as lemon juice and borax to leave your bathroom smelling fresh and sparkling clean.

2: Swap in new fixtures. It's amazing how much of a difference some gleaming new faucet handles will do for your bathroom's appeal.

3: Caulk gets worked away by the constant presence of water and moisture. It's very easy to replace, and it will help make our bathroom airtight, helping you avoid any damaging leaks caused by your shower or bath water. Remove old caulk with a utility knife, and be sure to clean any builtup mildew and soap scum before replacing it with new caulk.

MAKE A DRESSER INTO A BATHROOM VANITY

Recycle an old worn out dresser rather than sending it to the landfill—and add instant value to your home without spending a lot on a bathroom remodel. You can take this project to the next level by replacing the top of the dresser with a marble or stone countertop purchased from a salvage company.

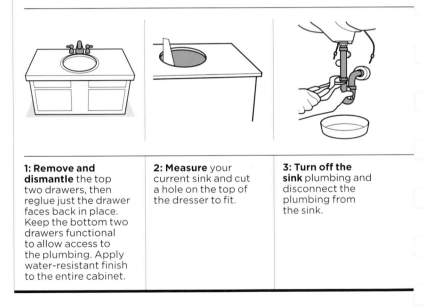

1: Remove and dismantle the top two drawers, then reglue just the drawer faces back in place. Keep the bottom two drawers functional to allow access to the plumbing. Apply water-resistant finish to the entire cabinet.

2: Measure your current sink and cut a hole on the top of the dresser to fit.

3: Turn off the sink plumbing and disconnect the plumbing from the sink.

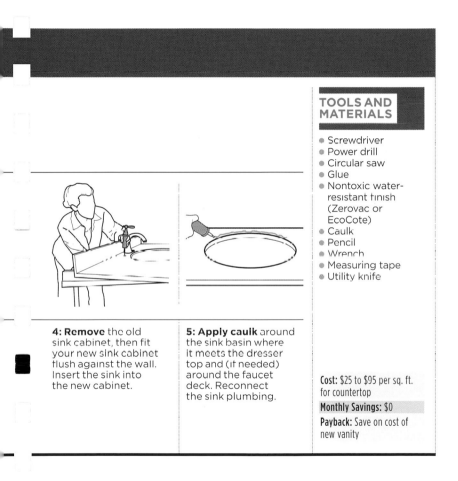

TOOLS AND MATERIALS

- Screwdriver
- Power drill
- Circular saw
- Glue
- Nontoxic water-resistant finish (Zerovac or EcoCote)
- Caulk
- Pencil
- Wrench
- Measuring tape
- Utility knife

4: Remove the old sink cabinet, then fit your new sink cabinet flush against the wall. Insert the sink into the new cabinet.

5: Apply caulk around the sink basin where it meets the dresser top and (if needed) around the faucet deck. Reconnect the sink plumbing.

Cost: $25 to $95 per sq. ft. for countertop

Monthly Savings: $0

Payback: Save on cost of new vanity

ON THE MOVE: CAR CARE

Since 1970, the number of cars registered in the U.S. has doubled, and Americans are keeping their vehicles longer. Because the motor fleet is so huge, if we continue to replace our vehicles at today's rate, it will take decades before we are all driving fuel-efficient vehicles. Even if you're not jumping on the hybrid bandwagon or converting your car to run on used vegetable oil, here are some simple ways to use less fuel and create fewer emissions.

TIPS OF THE TRADE
MINIMIZE IT!

OUR BEST ADVICE FOR REDUCING THE AMOUNT OF HAZARDOUS WASTE YOU NEED TO FIND A HOME FOR: REDUCE THE AMOUNT OF WASTE GENERATED, AND PLAN AHEAD TO MINIMIZE THE STUFF THAT HAS A FINITE SHELF LIFE.

- If you properly maintain your charging system, the battery will last longer.
- Buy only as much paint or solvent as you need for a project. If you'd done this all along, you wouldn't now need to dispose of a half-empty can for a car you haven't owned since the Reagan administration.
- Buy brake fluid in 8-oz. bottles instead of quarts to keep it from going bad.
- Keep your air cleaner fresh and well-sealed to prevent airborne dirt from contaminating your engine oil.
- Keep your suspension properly aligned and rotate your tires to reduce tread wear.

SMART FUEL

Americans burned through more than 142 billion gallons of gasoline in 2007—that's 16 million gallons per hour. Green alternatives to this expensive habit are slowly beginning to catch up to the market's demand. Here's a brief primer on where gasoline's alternatives stand today.

1: Diesel

While the cost of diesel (produced from petroleum) has skyrocketed, some of today's clean diesels can offer better fuel economy and produce fewer greenhouse gases than some gas/electric hybrids.

And because of how diesel engines are constructed, your diesel car will be around for a long time. It's not unusual to see diesel engines still chugging along at 250,000 miles.

2: Hybrid

Although hybrid electric vehicles come with a higher price tag than their gasoline equivalents, their high fuel economy, low CO_2 emissions, and federal and state tax credits should keep them high on your list. Some states offer perks to

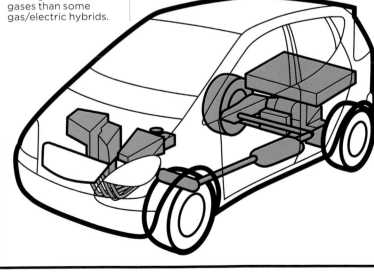

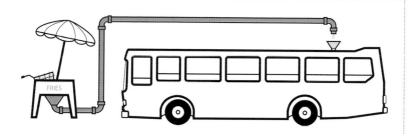

encourage hybrid use (for example, in New York, Florida, California, and Virginia, singly occupied hybrids are welcomed into HOV lanes).

3: Electric

The roadblock to functional electric vehicles has always been an energy-dense battery, but thanks to recent breakthroughs in lithium-ion technology, electric models are expected on the market in 2010. The downside? The estimated cost for a battery for a compact car that can achieve the 200-mile-range mark will be out of range for most buyers.

4: Hydrogen

The promise of hydrogen cars (zero emissions and high fuel efficiency) is tempting, but it will take years before the cost comes down to the level of a luxury car. Drivers may have to wait even longer for infrastructure that can deliver hydrogen when and where they want it.

5: Biofuel

The race to perfect a biofuel to replace gasoline began with corn-based ethanol. But while manufacturing vehicles to run on ethanol is relatively easy (there are roughly 60 models for 2008 that accept E85), recent studies revealed that biofuels derived from food crops are energy intensive and ultimately don't do much to alleviate climate change. Second-generation fuels (like biodiesel produced from algae) and those considered third generation (like renewable forms of gasoline and diesel) are still at laboratory scale.

6: Do It Yourself

If you're ready to make your own gas alternative, commercial processors won't come cheaply. Products such as the FuelMeister II and EFuel100 MicroFueler cost thousands of dollars and have limitations. A more wallet-friendly alternative are local initiatives such as the SFGreasecycle, which takes free vegetable oil waste from commercial enterprises and homes to be recycled as fuel.

RECYCLE

Recycling isn't just for cans and newspapers. You can recycle your car parts, too.

1: Fenders and More

There's a great after-market for handy car owners. Replace your damaged fender with a used one, and you will save and recycle a part already in existence.

2: Tires

There are organizations that will recycle your tires for free. Begin by contacting your local department of public works. It may use old tires to mix in with new road tar by grinding them up. Reklaim (reklaim.com) takes tires and recycles them into viable oil (one tire yields 1.37 gallons of oil).

Cost: $0

Monthly Savings: $0

Payback: Immediate

TIPS OF THE TRADE:
HOW TO REPLACE A FENDER

If you've located a new fender to replace your old, dented one—or have an aftermarket or OED fender—it's a simple do-it-yourself project. Modern basecoat/clearcoat paints make a professional refinishing job very easy with nothing more than an air compressor and spray gun, as long as you're willing to color-sand and buff out the finish once it's dry.

Even paint matching—once the bane of all would-be auto painters —is simple, thanks to the modern paint-matching equipment that many well-equipped auto stores have. Basecoat/clearcoat paints are extremely forgiving to apply. To choose the proper paint color, find the paint code, which is usually located on a doorjamb or the trunk lid. If you can't find the code, bring a piece of the car with the original paint—like the gas cap—to the paint store, where it can be matched by machine.

You may also need to take a utility knife and slice any seam sealer or undercoating that makes the fender adhere to the body. When lifting off the fender, take care not to scratch the door or hood.

To repair minor rust damage around bolt holes or where the fender contacts the body, clean the area with a wire brush. Then coat it with a chemical rust converter, available at auto parts stores. Once the converter is dry, paint the area with a zinc-rich primer from an aerosol spray can. Even if there's no damage to repair, take a few minutes to go over the area where the fender contacts the body with a wire brush. Any imperfection, dirt, or leftover seam sealer will prevent intimate contact between the new parts and the old—which may prevent the new part from fitting properly.

Install the fender by positioning it on the vehicle and holding it in place with several bolts that are loosely fastened. Most fender fasteners and their mounting points allow a certain amount of movement when loose to allow the fender to be adjusted for fit. Install all fasteners finger tight, then move the fender left and right and fore and aft to achieve an even gap at the door and hood seams while ensuring that the fender is flush with the body. After tightening all fasteners, double-check the fit and make sure the door and hood open and close properly. Leave any parts off the fender that will interfere with painting.

FINE-TUNING

Your vehicle will perform its best when it is properly maintained. A poorly tuned vehicle is likely to create more pollution and has a shorter life span. As a general rule of thumb, each of the following tune-up tasks should be completed every 7,500 miles.

1: Fuel Filter
A dirty filter can keep fuel from getting into the cylinders, which reduces fuel efficiency.

2: Spark Plugs
Spark plugs are needed to run effectively on all cylinders. When replacing spark plugs, calibrate them to factory specifications.

3: Air Filter
If your air filters aren't in good shape, dirt and debris can get into the engine of your car. Your car needs clean air to breathe.

4: Belts
The belts should be checked on a regular basis for cracks or tears. You need to replace the belts before they come apart, which is an expensive repair.

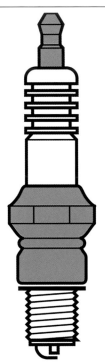

5: Fluid Levels
Check under the hood for fluid levels. Fluids include: brake fluid, power steering fluid, windshield wiper fluid, and coolant. Replace or fill as needed.

6: Battery
Terminals and connectors for the battery need to be kept clean. If you see dashboard lights fading or headlights faltering, you may have a problem.

7: Lights
Make sure all lights work, and not just to avoid a ticket. Other cars need to be able to see you to avoid hitting you. Check the headlights, taillights, turn signals, brake lights, and license plate lights.

8: PCV Valve
The PCV might cause your car to stall if it is plugged. Get it checked during the tune-up.

9: Tires

To get the best mileage out of your car, up the pressure to the maximum listed on the sidewall. The ride will get a bit rougher, but your rolling resistance will be reduced and you'll get better gas mileage. Make sure to check your tire pressure every other time you fill up, or you could be leaking air and losing MPGs.

10: Oil

Park your car on level ground when checking your oil level monthly. Consult your owner's manual and follow the recommendations (in order to stay within warranty). Oil keeps the moving parts of your motor lubricated and reduces friction—and don't forget to change the oil filter, which cleans the oil before it travels through your motor.

Cost: $400

Monthly Savings: $50

Payback: 8 months, save on replacement costs

KNOW YOUR STUFF:
WHAT'S THAT SMELL?

Remember that new-car smell? Actually, new cars haven't had that smell since manufacturers took the solvents out of the glues in the interior in an attempt to save a lot of UAW members' livers. Oh well. But there are plenty of other smells emanating from your car. Some of them are perfectly normal, even if they're annoying. Other odors are definitely evidence of Something Wrong. You—or your mechanic—can tell a lot about the source of an odor by simply walking around the car. Some odors are only apparent when the car is running, others when it's hot, others when it's sitting.

SMELLS LIKE: MAPLE SYRUP
When: After the engine has warmed or possibly even after it's shut off for a few minutes.

The Culprit: Coolant containing sweet-smelling (but toxic) ethylene glycol is leaking from somewhere. It could be coming from a radiator or heater hose or a failed intake manifold gasket or cylinder head. It might be coming from a leaky radiator cap or the radiator itself, especially if you smell it outside the car. A strong odor inside the passenger compartment probably means a bad heater core.

SMELLS LIKE: GYM SOCKS
When: You turn on the heater/air conditioner fan and you get a whiff of that high school gym locker.

The Culprit: It's good, old-fashioned mildew growing in the moisture condensing inside your A/C evaporator. And no, drizzling Listerine down the vents won't fix it, in spite of what your brother-in-law read on the Internet. Cheap solution: Turn off the A/C a mile from home and run the fan on high to dry the system out.

SMELLS LIKE: HELL
When: All the time, especially after the vehicle has been sitting after a long drive.

The Culprit: Yes, it really is brimstone, or, as it is usually called today, sulfur. This means gear lube is leaking from the manual transmission, transfer case, or differential housing. Sulfur compounds in this oil serve as extreme-pressure lubricants for the gears and can get pretty funky after a few years in service. Look for sulfury-smelling dribbles of viscous, oily stuff under the car. Unfortunately, leaks here typically mean a trip to the shop.

SMELLS LIKE: A GAS STATION

When: Parked, especially inside a garage or when the weather is really warm.

The Culprit: This is raw gasoline. On older cars—pre-1980 or so—some odor after is normal a hot shutoff from fuel after boil in the carburetor float bowl. Modern cars have an evaporative-emissions system that's tighter than our managing editor's deadline schedule, so any fuel smell means something is wrong. There may be a leak from a fuel-injection line or a fuel-tank vent hose.

SMELLS LIKE: ROTTEN EGGS

When: Any time your engine is running.

The Culprit: Hydrogen sulfide in the exhaust, which is produced by trace amounts of sulfur in gasoline. It's supposed to be converted to sulfur dioxide in your catalytic converter. This may be indicative of a fuel-injection problem and can be cured by a sharp mechanic. But often it means a failed catalytic converter. The bad news: a new cat is expensive. The good news is it's probably covered under warranty. Check with your dealer.

SMELLS LIKE: BURNT PAPER

When: At all speeds, particularly when you're working your way through the gears.

The Culprit: The clutch facing is burning off as the clutch slips. The odor is reminiscent of smoldering newsprint—like trying to burn the Sunday newspaper all at once in the fireplace, especially if it's been used to wrap sardines. The friction material is actually a paper composition, which explains the papery part of the smell. Either replace the clutch, or learn to stop riding the clutch pedal.

SMELLS LIKE: HOT OIL
When: Your engine is hot.

The Culprit: Oil is leaking onto the hot exhaust manifold. This is an acrid, burning smell. It's earthier and more nose wrinkling than the odor of cooking oil used for french fries. If it's from a leaky crankshaft seal that's spraying oil all over, some of it will find the red-hot manifold—but most will be on the pavement. A leaky valve cover won't necessarily leave a drip on the floor if all the oil drizzles onto the exhaust, vaporizing immediately. Look for smoke and try to stem the leak.

SMELLS LIKE: BURNT CARPET
When: After you've been using the brakes a lot, or hard, or both.

The Culprit: The brake pads are overheated. This is perfectly normal after riding the brakes coming down a long mountain pass—but you should learn to downshift, you flatlander. If you smell this under normal driving conditions, you've got a dragging brake caused by a seized-up brake caliper piston. Or maybe you just left the hand brake on. Check the temperature of the brakes by hand—the hot one is probably the smelliest.

FUTURE INVESTMENT

WHAT'S OLD IS NEW

A variety of options are available for retrofitting cars. These adjustments will make cars more efficient while lowering harmful emissions, although they are frequently pricy upfront. However, performing a retrofit means you can upgrade your vehicle and reuse it, rather than purchasing a new one.

1: Non Catalytic Syngas Generator

This technology enables diesel after-treatment system regeneration at lower temperatures and with less system complexity, resulting in lower capital and operating costs. (nxtgen.com)

2: Ultra-Low Emissions Combustion Technology

The low-swirl injector (LSI)

imparts a slight spin to the gaseous fuel and air mixture in a natural gas turbine, drastically reducing the level of emissions produced. It can also burn a variety of other fuels, such as hydrogen, and is easy to retrofit.

3: Greenbox

This device traps carbon dioxide and nitrous oxide, which are fed to algae and then crushed, producing a bio-oil that can be converted to biodiesel. The box needs to be replaced about every full tank of fuel.

4: EnviroFit

This technology allows two-stroke-powered vehicles to be retrofitted with cleaner, more efficient direct-injection technology. The upgrade improves fuel economy by as much as 30 percent. EnviroFit also eliminates 70 percent of carbon monoxide and 90 percent of hydrocarbon emissions. (envirofit.org)

QUICK FIX

GO WITH A FRIEND

Whenever possible, take public transportation, carpool, and combine your errands or activities into one trip. Find people to carpool with in your area on local or national sites such as RideSearch (ridesearch.com).

QUICK FIX

DON'T REV THE ENGINE

Whenever you start the engine, keep your foot off of the gas pedal. The simple act of revving the engine can take years off your transmission.

KNOW YOUR STUFF:
WHAT'S THAT SOUND?

A moving car is a complex symphony of sound, most of it reassuring—tires humming, engine rumbling, tailpipes roaring. But every now and then a dissonant note creeps into the mix—and the alert driver's ears prick up: Did you hear that? Here's a guide that identifies those oddball sounds and helps you sort out which conditions you can let slide and which ones mean repairs—and how fast you need to make them.

THUMPTHUMP
THUMPTHUMP
THUMPTHUMP

Where: From one or more tires.
When: At low speeds, especially in the morning; speeds up with car.
What: Flat-spotted tire. As the tire rotates, the flat spot thumps on the ground. Nylon-cord tires will flat-spot overnight and make this sound until they warm up. It's usually worse in colder weather. You can permanently flat-spot the tires by locking up the wheels, grinding massive amounts of rubber off the tread in one spot.
Urgency: Nada.

Fix: Replace your nylon tires with steel-belted tires. If you've ground down your tires like a pencil eraser, you can either live with the vibration until wear reduces the flat-spotting or buy new tires.

FFFFffff ttttFFFF ffff ttttFFFFffff tttt

Where: Under the hood.
When: Most noticeable at idle.
What: An exhaust manifold gasket has failed, venting hot exhaust gases to the air.
Urgency: It's not getting better on its own. The blowtorch of corrosive gases will eventually damage the manifold. Oh, by the way: carbon monoxide from the leak may make you drowsy or dead.
Fix: Replace the exhaust manifold gasket before the leak eats a hole in the manifold.

Ticktickticktick
Where: Under the center of the car, toward the rear.
When: While in motion and varying with road speed.
What: U-joint (rwd or 4wd only). A U-joint in your driveshaft has finally run out of grease, is getting loose, and is about to fail.
Urgency: That's really just an urban legend about cars pole-vaulting over broken driveshafts when U-joints fail at speed, right?
Fix: Replace all the U-joints and keep the new ones greased regularly.

EEEEEEEeeeee
Where: Inside the wheels.
When: Slowing down; it's sometimes worse on damp days.
What: Your brake pads are stroking the discs like a violin bow.
Urgency: Sometimes they do that. Your brakes still work fine.
Fix: Try new pads, adhesive to hold pads to the piston, or shims to insulate the piston from the pads. Another option: earplugs. (Sometimes the sound is difficult to eliminate.)

SSSSSSSSSSSS
Where: Under the hood.
When: Anytime the engine is running, but it's most noticeable at idle speed.
What: Vacuum leak. A rubber or plastic vacuum line or fitting has split or fallen apart.
Urgency: If you're wondering why your Check Engine light is on and why your car idles poorly, this is probably why.
Fix: Reconnect or replace the line.

Clang
Where: Under the center of the car or truck, near the middle.
When: Starting off at traffic lights. Most often heard on pickups with automatic transmissions, not manuals.
What: The splines that allow the driveshaft to change length where it connects to the tailshaft are binding as you slow down and then releasing when you start off.

(CONT.) KNOW YOUR STUFF:
WHAT'S THAT SOUND?

Urgency: Annoying, but *they all do that*—or at least some of them do it some of the time.
Fix: Packing the spline area with special grease helps for a month or so. Or just sell the car or truck.

ThunkThunkThunk
Where: One or both front corners of the vehicle.
When: Going around slow, sharp corners under light throttle.
What: A CV joint that allows your front wheels to turn and still be powered is loose. The boot has failed and let out all the CV joint's grease, or maybe it's just time for it to wear out.
Urgency: Don't leave town. Don't use a lot of throttle around sharp turns. Your car will stop suddenly when the joint completely fails.
Fix: Replace the entire off ending half-axle.

CLUNK
Where: Front end.
When: Initially, when parking; eventually, over small bumps.
What: The ball joint that connects the suspension arm to the upright has lost its lubrication and the metal-to-metal contact is wearing it out.
Urgency: Make an appointment. Avoid bumpy roads, curbs, and potholes.
Fix: Replace the ball joint.

GrumbleGrumble
Where: Front of the car.
When: At idle. (Check for weeping coolant at the bottom of the water pump, too.)
What: Water pump bearings.
Urgency: When the bearings fail completely, the fan will pull forward and slice a nice big smile-shaped chunk out of the radiator, making it leak profusely.
Fix: You need a new pump.

Yyyyoooooowwwwrrrrrrr
Where: Under the hood.
When: Whenever you rotate the steering wheel all the way to the left or right steering stop and hold it there.
What: The pressure relief valve inside the pump is dumping excess power steering hydraulic fluid back into the reservoir. It's supposed to do that, although maybe a little more quietly.
Urgency: No big deal.
Fix: It's normal. Actually, you should check the level of power steering fluid in the pump. Don't hold the wheel hard on the stop like that; it annoys pedestrians and is tough on the belt.

YEEEEeeeeeaaaaawwwppp
Where: Under the hood.
When: Right after startup until you rev the throttle a couple of times and the rubber warms up.
What: Belt squeal. A loose or glazed belt, bad tensioner, or misaligned pulley.
Urgency: Make an appointment, and don't take a long trip. This won't go away on its own—until just before the belt fails.
Fix: Check belt tension and pulley alignment; replace the belt.

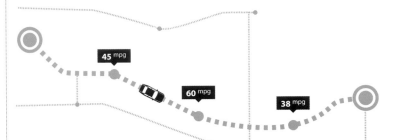

MONITOR YOUR FUEL ECONOMY

On the road, most drivers just read the trip odometer and divide by the amount of gas they purchase. But that doesn't account for differences in the driving cycle during each individual tankful. And that can vary an enormous amount. Your vehicle will get poorer fuel economy during the winter because of the increased electrical use for lights, wipers, heat, and longer warm ups. Spring and fall are even, but A/C use can certainly cause a mileage spike during the hot summer months. There are some tech tricks you can use to help monitor your fuel economy as you drive.

1: Scangauge is a $180 device that plugs into the On Board Diagnostic System (OBD II) port under the dash of virtually any post-1996 car or light truck. It operates as a scan tool so it gives you trouble codes and streaming data, but it also works as an electronic gauge cluster and trip computer. It tracks battery voltage, coolant temperature and sundry while tooling down the Interstate. But the instantaneous fuel economy readout is invaluable.

2: The CAMP2 from HKS is a scan tool/ gauge package/trip computer like the Scangauge, but it uses either the car's internal dashboard display or an aftermarket TV screen of any sort. It's intended to be professionally installed. Unlike the Scangauge, the CAMP2 has a graphic display that can be configured to reflect a dizzying number of parameters available from the vehicle's OBD II system. Input the car's weight and you can even get an instantaneous horsepower indication. You can look at raw numbers or at a simple analog-style gauge with a moving needle.

3: For a cheaper alternative, get an old-fashioned vacuum gauge at the local parts store. Monitoring manifold vacuum as you drive around will give you a fairly clear picture of your instantaneous fuel economy. BMW models have had a vacuum gauge integrated into the instrument panel for generations —it's simply labeled in miles per gallon instead of inches of vacuum. Higher manifold vacuum means higher mileage.

Cost: $15
Monthly Savings: $10
Payback: 2 months

QUICK FIX

GET GUIDANCE
The U.S. Environmental Protection Agency published the *Green Vehicle Guide* to help you choose the cleanest and most fuel-efficient vehicle that meets your needs. Low emissions and good fuel economy are good for you and for the environment. You can perform comparisons for up to three vehicles at one time. (fueleconomy.gov)

QUICK FIX

GAS ON THE CHEAP

With rising gas costs, everyone is looking to score a deal. But before you drive a few miles to the cheapest station, take a moment to weigh your potential savings against the cost of going the extra distance. You may spend more money burning fuel to get to your destination than you would save. The best way to save on gas is by stopping at the gas station with the lowest price on the route you take every day. Here are three great tools to keep you informed about where that is.

1: GasWatch. This PC download reports on the most recent data on gas prices in any requested area. (gaswatch.com)

2: GasBuddy. Enter your zip code and track the gas prices in your local area. Both GasBuddy and MOBGas send text message alerts to your phone. (gasbuddy.com)

3: GPS. Not only is a GPS a good way to spend less time driving in circles, some systems will give you the prices at gas stations in your area. However, a GPS comes with a hefty price tag itself—up to $1,000 or more.

QUICK FIX

FILL `ER UP
1: During warmer months, only fill your tank early or late in the day. This will reduce the amount of emissions that escape from your open tank.

2: Don't top it off. Stop filling your tank at the automatic shut off point. Overfilling your tank adds more evaporated emissions to the atmosphere, and you're paying for gas that simply evaporates away.

3: Go to the gas station between Monday and Thursday; stations can only increase the fuel cost once a week, and they often do so on Friday morning just before the weekend crowd.

QUICK FIX

DRIVE THE SPEED LIMIT
According to the U.S. Department of Energy, you pay an additional 15cents per gallon of gas for each 5 mph you drive over 60 mph.

GADGETS AND GIGABYTES

→ You can spend a small fortune trying to keep up with the latest technology. Cell phones, computers, and iPods become obsolete almost as soon as they are purchased. In this chapter you'll learn how to keep your aging gadgets useful with these easy projects. And if you simply have to have the latest release, these tips will keep your old gadgets out of the landfill.

↓ HOW MUCH JUICE DOES IT USE?

	ON	OFF
PLASMA TV	210 WATTS	1 WATT
CABLE BOX/DVR	26 WATTS	26 WATTS
DVD PLAYER	13 WATTS	2.3 WATTS
DESKTOP PC	80 WATTS	4.1 WATTS
LAPTOP	75 WATTS	2 WATTS
XBOX 360	173 WATTS	2.2 WATTS
SONY PS3	107 WATTS	1.3 WATTS
NINTENDO WII	16 WATTS	1.3 WATTS

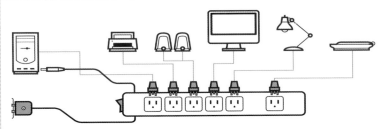

TURN ON AUTOPILOT

Many devices, including anything with a remote control or clock, continue to draw current when they're not in use. Consider how many electronic devices right now are plugged into an outlet at your home. Here are a few ways to cut back—or eliminate—the "phantom load."

1: Turn It Off. Shut down your PC if it will be idle more than two hours—this doesn't shorten its lifespan. Many devices (Xbox 360, e.g.) draw almost as much wattage standing idle as they do at work. Unplugging the device is even better.

2: USB Power Strips. This kind of power strip connects peripheral and other devices to your computer via a USB cable, and your electronics them draw their power through the computer. When your computer is off, everything plugged into a strip such as the Smart Strip Power Strip, including lights, PDAs, cell phone charger, and printers, cannot draw power from the current.

3: Programmable Timers. Some power strips are available with programmable timers to automate your device's use of electricity. Get a power strip with a built-in surge protector; even small surges of energy can cause permanent damage to your expensive equipment. Another choice is the Watt Stopper Isolé, which connects to an infrared occupancy detector and cuts off power if a room remains empty for several minutes.

4: DIY Automation System. For under $100, a DIYer can install a rudimentary system that controls certain lighting fixtures, A/C units, and an alarm system, and add devices to it over time. Be sure to buy components that work together—in typical electronics fashion, there are several competing standards, including Insteon, ZigBee, and Z-Wave Alliance.

5: Contractor-Installed Systems.

High-end systems can cost anywhere from $1,000 to upward of $10,000 tie together every circuit in the house, and allow for detailed control of all your electronic devices. By choosing "movie mode" on a PC keyboard, for example, a homeowner can adjust lighting, temperature, and perhaps the blinds for watching a video in the den—while turning down power in other rooms. Other high-end systems, such as an $11,000 setup by GridPoint, adjust electrical usage hour by hour based on utility pricing, incorporate backup batteries, and monitor energy production in homes equipped with solar panels and windmills.

Cost: $115 for three smart strips
Monthly Savings: $3
Payback: 3 years

QUICK FIX

PRINT LESS PAPER

The average office worker uses 10,000 sheets of paper each year, according to the EPA. Get in the habit of saving digital copies of e-mails, documents, and Web pages rather than printing them out. If you do need to print it out, and print on both sides of a page —and always recycle.

QUICK FIX

SOLAR CHARGED

The first solar cell made it into outer space aboard the first communications satellite in 1962. Now you can find a solar charger for practically any electronic item you have, including your phone, iPod, and laptop. When you factor in their savings, these chargers are well worth the investment.

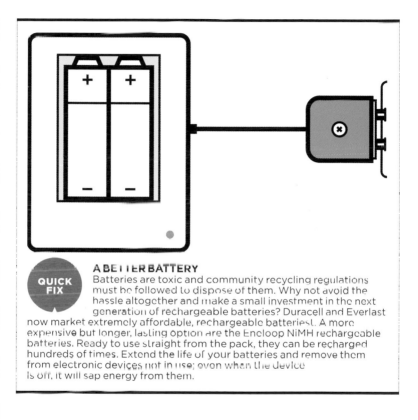

A BETTER BATTERY

QUICK FIX

Batteries are toxic and community recycling regulations must be followed to dispose of them. Why not avoid the hassle altogether and make a small investment in the next generation of rechargeable batteries? Duracell and Everlast now market extremely affordable, rechargeable batteries. A more expensive but longer, lasting option are the Encloop NiMH rechargeable batteries. Ready to use straight from the pack, they can be recharged hundreds of times. Extend the life of your batteries and remove them from electronic devices not in use; even when the device is off, it will sap energy from them.

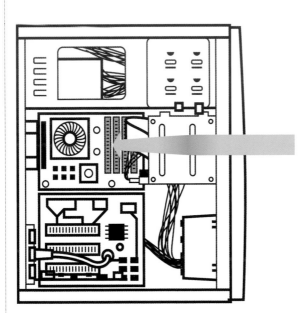

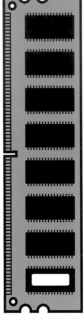

IMPROVE YOUR MEMORY

If your desktop computer is a few years out of date, consider upgrading its memory card before replacing it. You may not need a new computer after all. Before you open your computer's case, however, check to make sure this won't void your warranty.

1. Look through your computer's manual or check online at crucial. com or kingston.com to determine what kind of memory your computer requires.

QUICK FIX

You will either add a second RAM card or replace your old one. If necessary, bring your computer to a store for a consultation.

2: Unplug your computer. Ground yourself by touching an unpainted part of your computer case, then use the screwdriver or nut driver to open the case.

3. If you are replacing the old memory card, remove it now by working the clips located on its ends.

4: Insert the new memory by placing it in the slot at approximately a 45-degree angle and pushing it forward until it is perpendicular to the motherboard and the small metal clips at each end snap into place. Many slots do not have metal clips but instead rely on friction to hold the cards in place.

5: Close the computer case, plug it back in, and turn it on. Your computer should automatically recognize the new memory when it boots up.

TOOLS AND MATERIALS

- Your computer's manual
- New RAM (random access memory) card
- Screwdriver or nut driver

Cost: $115 for three smart strips
Monthly Savings: $3
Payback: 3 years

GENTLY WORN

Buy your electronics used from reputable company like Dyscern, which puts their refurbished electronics through extensive testing before reintroducing items on to the marketplace (dyscern.com). According the Silicon Valley Toxics Coalition, consumer electronics account for 70 percent of the heavy metals found in landfills.

KNOW YOUR STUFF:
SAVE MONEY ON PHONE LINES

If you still have a phone line at home, but use your cell phone for most of your calls, consider losing that monthly cost and use a voice over Internet protocol VOIP phone. Here's a closer look at Skype (technically a VoIP), which has some distinct advantages (and disadvantages) when compared with the established Internet phone services we've come to know and love.

	SKYPE	CONVENTIONAL VOIP
SETUP COST	FREE TO DOWNLOAD, FREE TO USE.	REQUIRES A SUBSCRIPTION PLAN. VONAGE, FOR INSTANCE, STARTS AT $15 PER MONTH; COMCAST DIGITAL VOICE STARTS AT $40 PER MONTH.
REQUIRED HARDWARE	TO TALK THROUGH YOUR PC YOU'LL NEED INTERNET ACCESS, A MICROPHONE, AND HEADPHONES OR SPEAKERS. NEW WIRELESS HANDSETS FROM RTX AND NETGEAR PLUG INTO YOUR COMPUTER AND ROUTER, RESPECTIVELY, LETTING YOU TAKE CALLS AROUND THE HOUSE.	VONAGE REQUIRES INTERNET ACCESS AND A VOIP HANDSET, WHICH COSTS AROUND $80. NO COMPUTER IS NECESSARY. WITH COMCAST, CUSTOMERS USE THEIR NORMAL PHONES WITH A PHONE ADAPTER THAT IS LEASED FOR $3 PER MONTH.
COST PER CALL	ALL CALLS TO OTHER SKYPE SUBSCRIBERS ARE FREE WORLDWIDE. SKYPE WORKS LIKE INSTANT MESSAGING, IN THAT BOTH THE CALLER AND RECIPIENT MUST BE LOGGED INTO THEIR ACCOUNT TO RECEIVE A CALL. PRICES ON PHONE CALLS TO ORDINARY PHONES VARY BY DESTINATION. (A CALL TO A LANDLINE IN FRANCE, FOR INSTANCE, COSTS 2 CENTS PER MINUTE.)	VONAGE'S CHEAPEST PLAN PROVIDES 500 MINUTES PER MONTH FOR IN-COUNTRY CALLS TO LANDLINES, BUT IN-NETWORK CALLS ARE FREE WORLDWIDE. A VONAGE CALL TO A FRENCH LANDLINE COSTS 4 CENTS PER MINUTE; ON COMCAST, ALL LOCAL AND LONG-DISTANCE CALLS ARE INCLUDED—A CALL TO UNCLE PIERRE IN BURGUNDY IS 9 CENTS PER MINUTE.

QUICK
FIX

QUICK
FIX

KILL SPYWARE

If your computer is used to browse the Internet, even if you scan your downloads automatically with antivirus software, it's likely you have spyware lurking in your system. These programs aren't simply limited to collecting personal information (such as your browsing history) but can install software, redirect your Web browser, access sites that may contain viruses, and even change your computer settings, resulting in the inability to connect to the Internet or slow connection speeds. Before your computer needs professional attention or you consider paying more for a faster Internet connection, try installing an anti-spyware program from a trusted source, such as Lavasoft's Ad-Aware (free for personal home use), Patrick Kolla's Spybot (free for noncommercial use), or Microsoft's Windows Defender (free).

TWO FOR ONE

Before you buy a new TV for your bedroom, consider salvaging one of the 250 million computers thrown away each year in the U.S. With a few minor upgrades and the installation of Slingbox, you can watch TV from the computer. (slingbox. com)

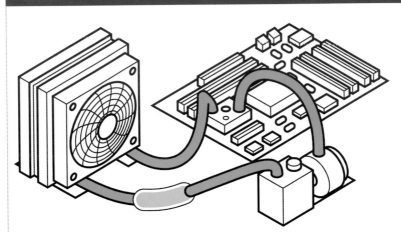

KEEP YOUR COMPUTER COOL

Water-cooled PCs run significantly cooler than fan-cooled PCs, and that will extend the life span of your computer. Fans are frequently under-powered and prone to collecting dust and dirt, which compromises their efficiency. A too-hot computer can melt the motherboard and the hard drive. If your computer is running hot, purchase a water-cooling kit and cool it off.

1: Do some research before you buy; kits are specific to your computer's motherboard. Some of the more popular brands available are Koolance, Thermatake, and Zalman.

2: Open the computer's case and unplug all cards and cables from the motherboard. Pull from the connector, don't tug on the wire. This will keep the two from ripping apart. Take careful note of the setup so you can reassemble everything later.

3: Remove the motherboard, then unclip and remove the heat sink. This is located in the center of the chip and will have a fan. Use a gentle twist-and-slide motion; the thermal paste already on the chip forms a tight bond. Clean the top of the exposed chip with an alcohol wipe and apply thermal paste (a conductive metal- or silicone-based grease included in the kit).

4: Install the water block using the mounting bracket provided. The mounting bracket will sandwich the motherboard with a bracket on the bottom and top connected with two screws. Don't over-tighten the screws.

5: Place the motherboard back into its case and reconnect all cables and cards. Use the supplied clamps to attach the hoses to the water block. If your pump and reservoir are separate components, you must run the hoses from one to the other and then into the radiator.

6: Now, hook up the pump's power cable to the connector coming from your PC's internal power supply. Check for leaks by filling the reservoir with the distilled water/coolant

mixture and priming the system.

TOOLS AND MATERIALS

- Water-cooling kit (includes a water block, hoses, pump, reservoir, and an external or internal radiator)
- Phillips screwdriver
- Flathead screwdriver
- Alcohol wipe

Cost: $100 to $200

Monthly Savings: $0

Payback: Save on cost of new computer

CLEAN UP
Don't underestimate the deteriorating power of dirt. Keep your electronic equipment clean—and more money in your pocket.

1: Desktop PC. Clean the exterior with a damp cloth. Inside the case, dust collects quickly and may restrict airflow. Remove the top or side panel and use a can of compressed air to blow dust from components such as the fans, CPU heat sink, and video card. Hold the can upright and position the case so its opening is in the direction you are pointing. This ensures dust will not resettle on your components.

2: Printer. The exterior may be cleaned with a damp cloth, but interior cleaning is different for inkjet and laser printers. Inkjets: Open the ink-cartridge access panel and use a dry cloth, foam, chamois cleaning swabs to remove any dust or ink. Then, run your printer's head-cleaning software to clear the ink nozzle. Laser printers: Remove the toner cartridge and wipe the toner cavity and rollers with a dry cloth. Avoid the transfer roller that sits directly under the cartridge. Don't wipe the optical mirror near the toner cavity; you'll only distort it.

3: Laptop. Use a 50/50 isopropyl alcohol and water mix to clean the laptop screen and a damp cloth on the shell and touchpad. Compressed air should be used to dust off the keyboard, ports, and fans—but first stick a toothpick in the fans so they won't be damaged. Consult your manual for instructions on how to detach the keyboard so you can dust the internal components. If your keys are soiled and if your manual indicates that they are removable, use cotton swabs and isopropyl alcohol to remove any residue.

4: Cell Phone. A soft cloth dampened with a 60/40 mixture of water and alcohol is the ideal way to wipe off your phone and

kill bacteria. If the keys are somewhat unresponsive (and if it won't void your warranty), follow instructions in your manual to pop open the front and rear panels and remove the battery and keypad. Use a swab dampened with undiluted alcohol to gently clean both the circuit board beneath the keypad and the power/data connector on the side or bottom of the phone.

5: Video Camera. For smudges on the lens, use a chamois cloth and a 50/50 alcohol/water solution. Many tape formats, such as MiniDV and Digital8, use internal lubricants that can form deposits on read/write heads and various rollers. If your image quality is suffering, run a

cleaning cassette through the camera for five to ten seconds. If the camera eats tapes, clean off any gunk on both the heads and capstans with an alcohol dampened swab, then allow them to air-dry before using.

6: TV. Using some commercial cleaners on your LCD or flat-panel screen will leave a residue, making the picture a little murky. Instead, make your own cleaner by combining one part alcohol and one part water in a spray bottle. Use a chamois cloth from your local hardware store and your screen will be dust and residue free.

TOOLS AND MATERIALS

- Can of air
- Toothpick
- Chamois cleaning swabs
- Rubbing alcohol
- Water
- Spray bottle

RESOURCES

CHAPTER 1

Web sites
The Daily Green
An online consumer guide to the green marketplace.
http://www. thedailygreen.com

Grist
Ideas and information about how to green your lifestyle.
http://www.grist.org

Books
Amann, Jennifer Thorne, Wilson, Alex, and Ackerly, Katie. *Consumer Guide to Home Energy Savings.* New Society Publishers, 2007.

Petersen, C. J. When *Duct Tape Just Isn't Enough: Quick Fixes for Everyday Disasters.* Hearst Books, 2007.

Scheckel, Paul. *Home Energy Diet: How to Save Money by Making Your House Energy-Smart.* New Society Publishers, 2005.

HEATING AND COOLING
Web sites
Energy Guide
Unbiased product and service information for everything from light bulbs to solar ovens.
http://www.energy federation.org

Energy Star
Government-sponsored site with tools and information for heating and cooling your home more efficiently.
http://www.energystar. gov

The Home Energy Saver
An online tool for calculating your energy use sponsored by the U.S. Department of Energy.
http://hes.lbl.gov

U.S. Department of Energy
Go directly to the source for the latest information and opportunities to reduce your energy use and save money in your home.
http://www.doe.gov

Books
The Editors of Popular Mechanics. *Plumbing & Heating.* Hearst Books, 2006.

The Editors of Popular Mechanics.

Weatherproofing & Insulation. Hearst Books, 2006.

Kemp, William H. *The Renewable Energy Handbook: A Guide to Rural Energy Independence, Off-Grid and Sustainable Living.* Aztext Press, 2006.

WATER
Web sites
American Rivers
Download a consumer guide to help you improve the quality of your local water supply.
http://www. americanrivers.org

Niagara Conservation
Practical and affordable products to help you conserve water in your home.
http://www.niagara conservation.com

Water Use It Wisely
Excellent resource for the many different was you can conserve watery in your specific region.
http://www.water useitwisely.com

Books
Becker, Norman. *Popular Mechanics 500 Simple Home Repair*

Solutions. Hearst Books, 2008.
Royte, Elizabeth. *Bottlemania: How Water Went on Sale and Why We Bought It.* Bloomsbury USA, 2008.

ELECTRICITY
Web sites
EPA's Clean Energy
The U.S. Environmental Protection Agency provides consumers with energy-efficient options available through local utility companies.
http://www.epa.gov/ cleanenergy/index.html

U.S. Fire Administration
Download a helpful tip sheet to help you avoid electrical fires in your home.
http://usfa.dhs.gov

Books
The Editors of Popular Mechanics. *Home Wiring.* Hearst Books, 2006.

Peters, Rick. *The Home How-to Handbook: Electrical, Tools, Techniques, and Quick Fixes.* Sterling Publishing 2006.

CHAPTER 2

Web sites
Built Green
Non profit environmentally friendly homebuilder's resource in Washington State with an excellent checklist of green building standards.
http://www.built green.net

Re-Nest
Eco-friendly home resources.
http://www. re-nest.com

Books
Coyne, Kelly, and Knutzen, Erik, *The Urban Homestead: Your Guide to Self-Sufficient Living in the Heart of the City.* Process, 2008.

Shim-Barry, Alex. *The Environment Equation: 100 Factors That Can Add To or Subtract From Your Total Carbon Footprint.* Adams Media, 2008.

Yudelson, Jerry. *Choosing Green: The Homebuyer's Guide to Good Green Homes.* New Society Publishers, 2008.

KITCHEN AND LAUNDRY
Web sites
Biodegradeable Store
Get your reuscable containers at this comprehensive shopping site that sells everything from sushi trays to doggy bags.
http://www.biode gradablestore.com

Kitchen Gardeners International
Promotes kitchen gardening, home cooking, and sustainable local food systems.
http://www.kitchen gardeners.org

Local Harvest
The go-to resource for finding locally produced food in your area.
http://www. localharvest.org

Steel Recycling Institute
Take recycled steel cans into your own hands and find locations in your area that will put your waste to good use.
http://www.sri.com

Books
Pleasant, Barbara, and Martin, Deborah L. *The Complete Compost Gardening Guide.* Storey Publishing, 2008.
Siegel-Maier, Karyn. *The Naturally Clean Home: 100 Safe and Easy Herbal Formulas for Non-Toxic Cleansers.* Storey Publishing, 1999.

BATHROOM
Web sites
AM Conservation Group
Purchase kits with everything you need to promote water conservation, including leak-detection dye tablets and water-efficient showerheads.
http://amcon servationgroup.com

GFX Technology
Online resource for heat-recovery systems for your home.
http://www.gfx technology.com

Books
Peters, Rick. *The Home How-To Handbook: Plumbing.* Sterling Publishing, 2006.

Peters, Rick. *MoneySmart Makeovers: Bathrooms.* Hearst Books, 2006.

LIVING ROOMS AND BEDROOMS
Web sites
Allergy Consumer Review
Great site for product reviews of vacuum cleaners, dehumidifiers, and other clean-air solutions for your home.
http://www.allergy consumerreview.com

Low-Impact Living
Many different green ideas and easy how-tos for your home.
http://www.low impactliving.com

Books
Hunter, Linda, and Halpin, Mikki. *Green Clean: The Environmentally Sound Guide to Cleaning Your Home.* Melcher Media, 2005.

BASEMENT AND GARAGE
Web sites
Consumer Reports
Gives you a brand by brand rating and comparison for furnaces.
http://www.consumer reports.org

Jay Leno's Green Garage
Green ideas and projects for

your garage.
*http://www.jay
lenosgarage.com*

Rubber-Cal
Eco-friendly and
affordable garage
flooring options.
*http://www.rubber
cal.com*

**U.S. Department
of Energy**
Download the *Solar
Water Heater Guide*
for detailed
descriptions of
products available
to homeowners.
http://ecre.doe.gov

Books
Peters, Rick. *Popular
Mechanics Garage
Makeovers: Adding
Space Without
Adding On.* Hearst
Books, 2006.

Staff of Stanley Books.
Complete Basements.
Stanley, 2006.

CHAPTER 3

ROOFTOPS
AND SIDING
Web sites
James Hardie
Nontoxic fiber cement
siding is long-lasting
and can save you big

bucks in maintenance
and replacement costs.
*http://www.
jameshardie.com*

Roofing.com
Excellent resource to
find roofing specialists,
services, and products
where you live.
*http://www.roofing
com*

Books
Dunnett, Nigel, and
Kingsbury, Noel.
*Planting Green Roofs
and Living Walls.*
Timber Press, 2008.

Earth Pledge
Foundation. *Green
Roofs: Ecological
Design and
Construction.* Schiffer
Publishing, 2004.

PATIOS AND
DRIVEWAYS
Web sites
Build It Solar
Multiple home
projects or those
wanting to go solar.
*http://www.build
itsolar.com*

EcoGreen
Based in Southeast
Asia, it has U.S.-based

operations and
provides a variety
of eco-products
from natural stone
to bamboo fencing.
*http://www.eco
greencompany.com*

Trex
If you want a deck
made out of recycled
milk jugs, this is where
you'll find one.
www.trex.com

Books
Davitt, Keith.
*Hardscaping: How
to Use Structures,
Pathways, Patios and
Ornaments in Your
Garden.* Sterling
Publishing, 2008.
Peters, Rick. *Popular
Mechanics MoneySmart
Makeovers: Porches,
Decks & Patios.*
Hearst Books, 2008.

LAWN AND GARDEN
Web sites
Beyond Pesticides
A nonprofit with a
comprehensive guide
to the dangers of
pesticides and what
you can do to lessen
your exposure.
*http://www.beyond
pesticides.org*

Clean Air Gardening
Environmentally friendly lawn and garden supplies.
http://www.cleanairgardening.com

NaturaLawn of America
Excellent resource for organic lawn care.
http://www.nl-amer.com

Rain Barrel Guide
How to use rain barrels in your yard or garden.
http://www.rainbarrelguide.com

Books
Becket, Ken, Bradley, Steve, Kingsbury, Noel, and Newbury, Tim. *Country Living Gardener Gardening Basics: How to Design, Plant & Maintain Your Garden.* Hearst Books, 2002.
Ludwig, Art. *The New Create an Oasis with Greywater.* Oasis Design, 2006.

CHAPTER 4

Web sites
Center on Sustainable Communities
Nonprofit educational resource for the residential home market with the latest trends and resources for the individual homeowner.
http://www.icosc.com

Pro-Teck
This Connecticut-based company will haul away local remodeling waste, including paint, asbestos, and underground oil tanks, and it'll dispose or recycle everything sustainably. If you aren't local, it will provide a referral for your area.
http://www.proteckllc.com

Renovation Experts
Search thousands of home contractors and experts in your specific area.
http://www.renovationexperts.com

Sustainable Buildings Industry Council
Non profits with information about materials and regulations in the green building industry.
http://www.sbicouncil.org

U.S. Green Building Council
Nonprofit organization with comprehensive information and resources to make green buildings available to everyone.
http://www.usgbc.org

Books
Jackson, Albert, and Day, David. *Popular Mechanics Home Repairs & Improvements.* Hearst Books, 2006.

Johnston, David, and Gibson, Scott. *Green from the Ground Up: Sustainable, Healthy, and Energy-Efficient Home Construction.* Taunton Press, 2008.

Rooney, E. Ashley, Hartke, David, and McConnell, John C. *Green Homes: Dwellings for the 21st Century.* Schiffer Publishing, 2008.

FLOORS
Web sites
Sustainable Flooring
Specific products like cork and bamboo flooring are available, but this is also an excellent source of information about where to go for sustainable building information in general.
http://www.sustainableflooring.com

TerraMai
Reclaimed wood
products from around
the world, with
some great savings
opportunities on
specific products.
*http://www.terramai.
com*

Books
Bennett, Clayon. *Black
and Decker: Complete
Guide to Floor Decor.*
Creative Publishing
international, 2007.

Siegenthaler, John.
*Modern Hydronic
Heating for Residential
and Light Commercial
Buildings.* Delmar
Cengage Learning,
2003.

WALLS
Web sites
American Clay
Environmentally
friendly alternative
to cement, gypsum,
acrylic, and other
toxic materials.
*http://www.
americanclay.com*
Old Fashioned
Milk Paint
Eco-friendly, nontoxic
paint for your home.
*http://www.milkpaint.
com*

Books
Binggeli, Corky.
*Materials for Interior
Environments.*
Wiley, 2007.

Wilson, Alex,
Piepkorn, Mark, and
Malin, Nadav. Green
*Building Products: The
Greenspec Guide to
Residential Building
Materials.* New Society
Publishers, 2008.

KITCHEN
Web sites
ApplianceXchange
Upgrade your kitchen
with slightly used,
discontinued, or retail
overstock appliances.
*http://www.applianc
exchange.com*

Low Impact Living
has a listing of
resources in different
areas for supplies
and advice for your
remodeling project.
*http://www.low
impactliving.com*

Books
Peters, Rick. *Popular
Mechanics MoneySmart
Makeovers: Kitchens.*
Hearst Books, 2007.

WINDOWS
Web sites
Efficient Windows
Collaborative
Unbiased information
about energy-efficient
windows and the
various options
available.
*http://www.efficient
windows.org*

Books
Lawrence, Mike.
*DIY Guide to Doors,
Windows, & Joinery.*
Crowood Press, 2007.

CHAPTER 5

Web sites
Auto Blog Green
Expensive industry
information on the
latest technologies
and newest models
available to the energy
conscious driver.
*http://www.
autobloggreen.com*

Edmunds
The best consumer
resource for cars now
has an entire section
dedicated to helping
you chose smarter
energy-efficient cars.
*http://blogs.edmunds.
com/greencaradvisor/*

Gas 2.0
Everything you will ever want to know about biodiesel and more.
http://gas2.org

Hybrid Cars
Buyers guide, mileage calculator, and more on this informative Web site dedicated to all things hybrid.
http://www.hybrid cars.com

Rand McNally
You don't have to know how to read a map to use this site. You can send everything from information about traffic to road construction straight to your wireless device or your GPS system. You'll save time, gas, and money.
http://www.rand mcnally.com

Ron Cogan's GreenCar.com
For the car-obsessed, this site covers all angles of the eco-friendly car market.
http://www.green car.com

U.S. Department of Energy
Tools and facts to help you save money and fuel.
http://www. fueleconomy.gov

Books
Editors of Popular Mechanics. *Complete Car Care Manual.* Hearst Books, 2008.

Freudenberger, Bob. *Popular Mechanics Car Owner's Companion.* Hearst Books, 2006.

CHAPTER 6

Web sites
Consumer Electronics Organization
Commonsense solutions to reducing your e-waste.
http://www.mygreen electronics.org

Consumer Reports
Find out which new products are worth the money.
http://www.consumer reports.org

Electronic Recyclers International
Find out where to send your old gadgets from the largest e-waste recycler in the U.S.
http://www.electronic recyclers.com

EPEAT
Electronic Product Environmental Assessment Tool.
http://www.epeat.net

Green Batteries
The ultimate one-stop shopping resource for eco-friendly batteries.
http://www.green batteries.com

Greenpeace Guide to Greener Electronics
An annual snapshot of where the top electronic companies stand on green initiatives.
http://www.green peace.org/electronics

INDEX